WEST OF JESUS

By the same author

The Angle Quickest for Flight

WEST OF JESUS

SURFING, SCIENCE AND THE ORIGINS OF BELIEF

STEVEN KOTLER

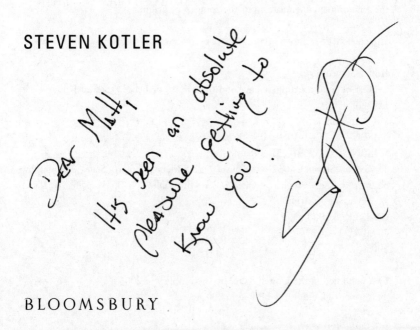

Dear Matt!
It's been an absolute
pleasure getting to
know You!

BLOOMSBURY

Portions of the book have appeared in *Men's Journal, Discover, GQ, LA Weekly* and *Blue*.

Excerpt from "Water" from *Collected Poems* by Philip Larkin. Copyright © 1998, 2003 by the estate of Philip Larkin. Reprinted by permission of Farrar, Straus, and Giroux, LLC.

Published by Bloomsbury USA, New York

All papers used by Bloomsbury USA are natural, recyclable products made from wood grown in well-managed forests. The manufacturing processes conform to the environmental regulations of the country of origin.

THE LIBRARY OF CONGRESS HAS CATALOGED THE HARDCOVER EDITION AS FOLLOWS:

Kotler, Steven, 1967–
    West of Jesus : surfing, science and the origins of belief / Steven Kotler.—1st U.S. ed.
        p. cm.
    ISBN-13: 978-1-59691-051-5 (hardcover)
    ISBN-10: 1-59691-051-8 (hardcover)
1. Kotler, Steven, 1967– —Travel. 2. Surfers—United States—Biography.
3. Lyme disease—Patients—United States—Biography. 4. Spiritual life. I. Title.

GV838.K68 2006
797.3'2092—dc22
2005032552

First published in the United States by Bloomsbury in 2006
This paperback edition published in 2007

Paperback ISBN-10: 1-59691-344-4
ISBN-13: 978-1-59691-344-8

10 9 8 7 6 5

Typeset by Westchester Book Group
Printed in the United States of America by Quebecor World Fairfield

PART ONE

This is the real world Muchachos, and we are all in it.

—Charles Bowden

1

In *The White Album,* Joan Didion wrote, "We tell ourselves stories in order to live," and then proceeded to tell a story about a time in her life when the stories she told herself began to fail. Which may be how things go for many of us, and it certainly was for me. In the fall of 2003, at a time when I was making my living as a journalist; at a time when the president of the United States comfortably dismissed the idea of Darwinian evolution in favor of a more economic, six-day approach; at a time when certain members of Congress were trying to remake democracy in their own image; at a time when I was recovering from a long and nagging illness; when many of the people around me began getting married, having children, moving away, or on, or staying exactly where they were, without me; at a time a pair of hurricanes were heavy on the neck of Central America, I went to Mexico to surf. I went because of these things. I went because the stories I told myself had begun to fail.

Owing to the long illness, it had been too long since I'd been someplace tropical. In the years prior, I had spent chunks of my life in far-flung places. When friends asked why I went, I ticked off a long list of mildly verifiable purposes. The truth of the matter was I went to such places because most people didn't. On a map and in reality, such places are hard to get to and far away. I wanted to be the kind of person who went places hard to get to and far away. I was interested in places that are far away on maps, just as I was interested in places that are far away in reality. I didn't know then, not like I know now, that such places do not always coincide.

I was afraid of such journeys and took them anyway. Mexico was almost this kind of quest. Not that my trip there was arduous by anyone's measure. A three-hour flight followed by an hour car ride. The ride was bumpy, but that doesn't count. I was going to a place called Costa Azul, which does not mean, as I was disappointed to find out, "the Blue Cost."

The bitch of it was my suitcase. For starters my suitcase was eight feet long. I take pride in traveling light, so finding myself dragging eight feet of dead weight was embarrassing in a privately psychological way. Plus, owing to the long illness, my time away from the tropics and a seeming predisposition toward exertion, I packed wrong. It was almost a hundred degrees in Mexico. I packed three T-shirts, two pairs of shorts, two sweatshirts, one jacket, two wetsuits, three sweaters and two surfboards. I promised myself that I would do no work in Mexico and then brought fifty magazines, mostly back issues of the *Economist* and the *New Scientist,* and a handful of books, including David Quammen's wonderful *Monsters of God,* about "man-eating predators" and these, their final years on Earth. I took these things because I cared about things like economists, new scientists, tigers. I cared about what happened when the very things humans built myths around began to fail. My bag weighed a fucking ton.

I went to Mexico because I had spent the summer working as hard as I can remember working while realizing that my life had somehow developed a heavy glass ceiling that I was constantly slamming my head against. I was thirty-six years old, a citizen or at least a taxpayer, in need of a new couch, fully capable of making green beans in the Szechuan style, single, not especially lonely, plagued by junk mail, attached to the words of Ernest Hemingway:

"The world breaks everyone and afterwards many are stronger at the broken places." I was a little amazed that life was nothing more than an accumulation of days. I was suffering that same disjointed feeling that many my age seem to suffer: life was not going to be anything other than what I made it.

If I chose to stay home and watch television, I was choosing not to do something else. I once drove a car with a KILL YOUR TELEVISION bumper sticker on it. It felt like lifetimes ago, many lifetimes ago. Now I lived in Hollywood and had developed an unnatural attachment to *The West Wing*. One of the things I learned watching *The West Wing* is that if you combine the populations of Great Britain, France, Germany, Japan, Switzerland, Sweden, Denmark and Australia, you'll get a population roughly the size of the United States, where, last year, there were 32,000 gun deaths. Those other countries, which all have a form of gun control, had a total of 112.

In the course of my life I've had four handguns waved in my face, been caught in automatic weapon's crossfire on three other occasions and was once muzzle slammed with an AK-47 by an Indonesian soldier in a Balinese nightclub after a deejay decided to play punk rock and we decided to slam dance—apparently a crime in that country. I've also known more than my fair share of people who have been on both sides of a firearm. Two come to mind. The first was a professional skier who took a random sniper's bullet through his windshield and then his lung while driving through the Sierra Nevada. The second was an enforcer for the Hell's Angels. He was a small guy, a fact I found surprising since being an enforcer for the Hell's Angels seemed to be a job that would require some mass. He once told me that he was good at his job because he was willing to do more damage than anyone thought possible. The last I heard he had rolled his van while crossing the Arizona desert. When the cops came to extract him from the wreckage, they found enough firepower to start a small war in a small country.

I can say that at the time I went to Mexico I was thirty-six years old and the things I was choosing not to do were starting to add up into a whole other life I was choosing not to live.

2

In September of 2000, I was living with my girlfriend in an apartment in Los Angeles. The apartment and the girlfriend were both beautiful. I wanted, desperately, for them to be both my dream apartment and my dream girl, but in both cases—as it turned out—the rent was too steep. When people asked me exactly where in Los Angeles my apartment was, I would say Beachwood Canyon, and when they inevitably asked where Beachwood Canyon was, I would tell them that when an earthquake finally shook free those bold letters of the HOLLYWOOD sign, the *H* would crush my living room. That was not the truth. Beachwood Canyon runs for miles, and the HOLLYWOOD sign looms like a gargoyle at the top. I lived near the bottom. I never thought of this line as a lie; I just thought of it as a way to make things simpler. It was a complicated couple of years, and simpler seemed a reasonable choice considering everything else there was to consider.

I had found out, in this apartment, with this girlfriend, in early April, that I had Lyme disease. By late September, after six months on strong medicine, I was still waking up each morning too exhausted to get out of bed; or I could get out of bed but actually making it to the kitchen for coffee was an impossible task, so I would lie down on the floor, at about the place I realized such things, because I didn't have the strength to do anything else. We had louver windows in that apartment, and there's a lot of dust in Los Angeles, and much of that dust blew in our windows and ended up on our floor. I spent a lot of time on that floor, and much of that time was spent with the T. S. Eliot line "I'll show you fear in a handful of dust" stuck in my head.

There were also days when I could make it out of bed and to the kitchen to make coffee, but my brain—owing to the neurological assault that distinguishes Lyme—would forget how to make coffee and I would stand with the pot in one hand and the tap running, not sure of what to do next; or I would remember and start making coffee, but owing to the effect the disease had on my vision, I would suddenly find myself unable to see the coffeepot, the running water, the floor I stood upon, and would have to grope around and go slow or risk pouring water into another toaster. That year, I was hell on appliances.

During this time I kept a notebook beside my computer that contained some simple instructions.

1. To turn on the computer, push the smaller of the two round buttons.
2. You have DSL. If the computer is already on, you are already connected to the Net; if not, go to the folder under the Apple menu and click CONNECT.
3. Wear socks—there's a chill in the room.
4. Socks are those long cloth things with a hole in one end and no hole at the other. They're in the second drawer from the top, in the dresser, in the bedroom.
5. Remember to feed the dog; remember the dog is that furry thing sitting near your feet.
6. Remember that you've forgotten how to spell and, for the most part, your grammar now sucks.
7. Remember that you've most likely forgotten that you've forgotten how to write as well, so the difficulty you've been having is perfectly normal and preferably should not result in violence, again.

8. Try not to panic, complain or daydream.

9. Keep passing the open windows.

A number of these entries were absolutely necessary for daily living. A number were there to help me stay in a good mood. The last two were the most critical. Panic was a near constant that year, but owing to the fact that Lyme has a built-in stress trigger—meaning the more stressed out I became, the sicker I felt, and the sicker I felt, the more stressed I became—it was the exact kind of surrealistic hilarity that was best avoided. Trying not to complain was almost as hard, but I was committed to being ill with some grace and I was attempting to hold my relationships together with hat pins and twine—and failing miserably on both counts. Trying not to daydream was important because I would often emerge from my daydreams to realize that my life had little to offer by way of comparison, which might be the way of such things, but it didn't make it any easier. The final line was from John Irving's *The Hotel New Hampshire*. The reason you wanted to keep passing the open windows was to keep from eventually jumping out of one.

It was on a day in September that I realized my list was not at all different from the list employed by characters suffering through the plague of amnesia that infects the town of Macondo in Gabriel García Márquez's *One Hundred Years of Solitude*. The plague eventually becomes so bad that townsfolk begin leaving notes pinned to various and important items to remind everyone of their purpose: "This is the cow. She must be milked every morning." It is an interesting experience to find yourself living inside one of your favorite scenes from one of your favorite books, more so when the scene in question is often held up as one of the examples of why the book is considered magical realism. This is especially interesting when you consider that they call it magical realism because of its supposed impossible and fantastic nature.

3

Along similar lines, here are a few of the diseases people thought I had before anyone figured out I had Lyme: the flu, the Chinese flu, sinusitis, mad cow, malaria, giardia, schistosomiasis, lymphoma, lupus, leukemia, leishmaniasis, anemia, AIDS, the common cold, strep throat, sleeping sickness, schizophrenia, rheumatoid arthritis, clinical depression, road rage, low thyroid function, chronic fatigue syndrome and White Shaker Dog Syndrome which, as it turns out, is mainly found in cocker spaniels.

Owing to certain legal entanglements resulting from my insurance company's desire not to pay my medical bills, there is very little I can say about this topic. I can say that before I got sick I had taken a job as a staff writer at a magazine, and it was a job that I had chased for over a decade. I can say that while ill I lost certain things: that job, a woman, much of my mind, years of my life. These are things that I have gotten beyond, without much fanfare, in the way people get beyond such things.

About the same time I got sick, a good friend of mine did as well. He was both my rock-climbing partner and married to a devout Christian Scientist. He suffered a brain aneurysm while working his way up a difficult climb, some forty feet above the ground. In the emergency room, he was confronted by two distinct emergencies. The first was a doctor telling him he was very lucky to be alive and that if he stayed very still for a long time he just might get to stay that way. The second was his wife telling him that if he did not immediately get out of bed, leave the hospital and put his recovery into the hands of God, she would be forced to divorce him. The saddest song lyric I know is "she said she'd stick around 'til the bandages came off." Tom Waits sang it. My friend's wife didn't even stick around that long.

I am now thirty-eight years old and often find a direct and peculiar conflict between my personal mythology and the real world.

4

I knew nothing about Costa Azul. A week prior to my departure I was informed by an editor that a story I had spent many of the previous months writing and researching would not be published. This was something that happened occasionally in my journalism career. Historically, about once every three years. Sometimes it meant I wasn't writing well; sometimes it meant an editor wasn't editing well. There were times when the story under investigation turned into a completely different story as the events played out, and this second story turned into something far less interesting than the first. Occasionally, a story that was tied to a news peg got trumped by other, more important news; or the decision not to publish it represented a managerial shift in editorial content, which had the magazine sailing in a new direction while the assigned story still belonged to that older one. For all these reasons, it helped to take such things in stride.

Not three hours after that first editor called, my phone rang again. It was another editor from another magazine calling to inform me that another story I had spent many of the previous months writing and researching would not be published. The next morning I was informed by a third editor at a third magazine that a third story I had spent many of the previous months writing and researching would be delayed and most likely have to be radically rewritten if it had any chance of publication. This was not the usual course of events.

There's a lot of fear involved in long illness, a bunch of time spent wondering how much of the old life has been lost, how small of a future are we now talking about. I surfed and I wrote, and that was the extent of things. A lot of days I was too sick to surf. Those three articles disappeared in less than twenty-four hours. I hung up the phone after that last phone call wondering where my life had gone.

My dog is named Ahab. He's half rottweiler and half husky and looks like a black-and-brown version of a panda bear. A few years prior he had shown up on a friend's doorstep and refused to leave. At that time he did not look like a black-and-brown panda bear. His ample coat had knotted into a solid dreadlock, and there were cigarette burns trailing down his back. He looked like someone had tortured a Rastafarian and then magically transformed what little was left into a dog. In the period of time that I am talking about, I began hiking with Ahab in Griffith Park during the middle of the night. If I was writing a book titled *Dumb and Dangerous Things to Do in Los Angeles,* hiking Griffith Park at night would be in the first chapter, but back then it was one of the few things that made any sense to me. On the drive to these hikes I would play Radiohead's "Karma Police." I was amazed by Thom Yorke's ability to take a seemingly simple phrase and sing it repeatedly during a song, allowing it to accrue meaning as it went. I was obsessed with "Karma Police," with the pertinent line "For a minute there, I lost myself, I lost myself." I am undeniably tone-deaf. I would sing in my car and sing on the trail. I would do so at the top of my lungs. I lost myself. I lost myself. If you don't believe me, just ask my dog.

I am telling you these things because it may help explain what happened next. What happened next, at least in the next that immediately followed the phone call from my third editor, was that I poured myself a small glass of bourbon and started staring out my apartment window. This being California, there was a palm tree across the street from my window. There was a man forty feet up in the palm tree, just below the fronds. He had wrapped what appeared to be twine around his waist and around the tree trunk. I had seen landscapers in Ecuador do the same thing with thick rope. They would use the rope for leverage and stability as they ascended the tree to trim dead branches. In Ecuador, the landscapers would climb with a small saw clenched between their teeth like a pirate with a dagger. The man across the street from me didn't have a saw, nor did he appear a pirate. In fact, he appeared to be sixty years old, twenty feet off the ground and staring at the sky. He did not move for a long time. Then he slid down and walked away. Apparently, he had only come for the view.

It had been a long time since I had been anywhere with a view. Before he had reached the street corner I picked up the receiver and made a phone call to a travel agent I had never heard of before, whom I found on a Web site I had never visited before. The Web site specialized in surf travel. On the site are pictures of those perfect waves one finds on Web sites that specialize in surf travel. These are waves the vast majority of surfers will say they have never seen, but maybe it was time to try. When all else fails, I thought, go on a damn quest.

This was not, particularly, a rational decision. I had not traveled far in four years because I could not predict which days I would bound out of bed energetic or which days I would never leave at all. Waves with long arms raised some very mixed feelings. I told the agent that I wanted to leave the country, surf every day, read and perhaps, occasionally, have a conversation. She told me I was going to Costa Azul.

5

It was a crisp seventy degrees when I left California and a gummy ninety when I landed in Puerto Vallarta. Navigating the crowded airport with my surf bag was about as much fun as drowning. Forty yards from baggage claim a man reached out and grabbed my wrist. He could have been thirty years old; he could have been sixty years old. He wore a baby blue suit and baby blue shoes and a white shirt with rhinestones studding the collar. Urgently, he demanded I put down my bag. Owing to the fact that my brain had not yet decided it was time to speak Spanish again, it took a little while to understand why it was as such.

"He's coming" is what he said over and over again.

I had prearranged a ride from the airport to Costa Azul and considered that he might be talking about my driver. I tried to tell him my driver was meeting me on the other side of customs, which I had yet to clear.

"El hombre espera otra lado del costumbre" is what I tried. Unfortunately, a number of words in that sentence, my Spanish-English dictionary told me later, meant something else. The literal translation of what I was saying was "my driver is waiting across my habit." Which might have been the case as well, but the man kept shaking his head against it.

"He's coming," he said again.

"Who?" I repeated. "Who's coming?"

"From there," he said finally, exasperated, pointing to a spot in the airport's roof which looked liked a coffee stain on a white couch. "He's coming from there."

On the other side of customs my driver was waiting. He welcomed me to Mexico and led me out into the sunshine. We crossed the parking lot, on the way to an old pickup truck the color of rotting avocados. Mud splatters coated the tires, fanning out across the sides. Plastered to the rear was a bumper sticker. It read: JESUS IS COMING: LOOK BUSY. This was a level of religious irony not often found in Catholic countries. This was a level of coincidence about which I have not been properly trained to comment.

One of the largest and most expensive shopping malls in America is found in Palo Alto, California, near Stanford University. Years before, several friends and I had printed up several thousand small stickers reading: WE ARE EVERYWHERE. We had driven to this mall during a holiday weekend and attached stickers to every bumper we saw. A few days later a small segment of the local television news was devoted to the mysterious plague of bumper stickers mysteriously plaguing Palo Alto. In closing, the newscaster, with a level of irony not often found on local news, said, "The question remains—who are we?"

It is almost fifteen years later, and I still think it's a fair question.

6

Costa Azul is an "adventure resort" which, being found in Mexico, has probably seen more than its fair share of adventure. It's located in the state of Nayarit, near the village of San Blas, about which the poet Henry Wadsworth Longfellow wrote "The Bells of San Blas." The poem contains the lines "Oh, bring us back once more, the vanished days of yore, when the world with faith was filled." Coincidentally, San Blas is where Father Junipero Serro began his northward journey, spreading Catholic gospel up the long spit of land that would eventually become California.

The resort is a few miles down the road from San Blas, in the village of San Francisco. Since Saint Francis is known in parts of Mexico as Pancho, the town of San Francisco is known locally as San Pancho. In 1970, the former president Luis Echeverría Álvarez took a proprietary interest in San Pancho, installing a series of high-minded amenities. For the first time ever the town had running water, public schools and a hospital. Supposedly, Echeverría Álvarez had hoped to receive a prestigious United Nations posting by creating in San Pancho a self-sufficient town that would be a model for Third World development. The only information I can track down on his fate says that things did not work out as planned.

The road that winds into San Pancho is a thin twist of dirt and gravel, banked by lush, undulating terrain. In the distance are remote hilltops where old-growth trees still stand tall. Closer to the road, the forest had been pillaged for tropical hardwoods, but enough time has passed between then and now that a new canopy has regrown, thick and labyrinthine. Cows and horses graze in this tangle and occasionally wander across the roads. Just back from the gravel shoulder are dozens of wooden, white markers where—one suspects—cows have wandered and cars have swerved and things have gone badly for all concerned. Mexicans believe that the soul lingers in the spot where death occurred until proper tribute has been paid. Funerals held in villages far away are not enough, so this road is lousy with crosses.

San Pancho is a small, coastal, fishing village hacked from the edges of the jungle. The residents are farmers or fishermen or both. It is not unusual to find senior citizens wearing cowboy hats and riding donkeys through the streets. There are a few shops, a half-dozen restaurants and a main church with a tall white steeple. The church sits in a small cobblestone plaza. Once a year, the locals throw a weekend festival here. The music is live, and people come from miles. At the height of the festival, at around midnight on Saturday, when everyone's drunk seventeen or eighteen of whatever it is they are drinking, a bull is let loose in this plaza. Before the animal is released, its torso is wrapped in fireworks and the fuse lit. The result is a low-rent running-with-the-bulls spectacle with an apparently acceptable level of carnage. Occasionally, someone is gored. Occasionally, a small white cross is added to the main square. This is what passes for fun in San Pancho.

The coastline that runs from Puerto Vallarta north to Santa Cruz is a giant, curving bay, dotted with some of the better surf spots in mainland Mexico. In San Pancho proper the one decent wave is a rivermouth break. In some such breaks, like Malibu and Rincon, the outflowing river forms alluvial sandbars that flawlessly shape incoming waves with such consistency that the rides there have become the stuff of dreams. San Pancho is not that kind of rivermouth. It's shallow and mean and runs over a persnickety rock bottom that requires a rare and sizable north swell to work. All rivermouths are heavy with pollutants and agricultural runoff and the flotsam of upstream, inland living, but Mexican rivermouth breaks are dirtier than most and often thick with sharks. For these reasons San Pancho has yet to develop the heavy surf tourism of neighboring towns. Costa Azul is the only hotel around and stays busy primarily because the owner is a San Diego native with a decent advertising budget and because the staff uses boats and cargo vans to ferry guests to the best waves around.

The resort sits a few miles outside of town. It's a multitiered complex that starts high on a hilltop and works its way a few hundred yards down to the beach. High up on that hill are the more expensive condo-style rooms. Down low are smaller rooms and a small concrete office and beyond that a sprawling bar and restaurant, built under a giant thatched roof. It is a kind of Tiki hut writ large. There are no walls. On one side of the bar is a swimming pool shaped like a pear; on the other side is the beach shaped like a beach.

By the time I checked into my room, it was about three in the afternoon and the sticky ninety-degree heat had climbed to over a hundred. I threw on a pair of board shorts and joined about ten other guys in the swimming pool. Very few women actually come to Costa Azul. The ones who do come with boyfriends or husbands or boyfriends who will soon be husbands. That day, like most, the pool was empty of estrogen.

I wanted to know how the surf was—which is what surfers on vacation always want to know, though most surfers on vacation want to know that the surf is booming. In general, in October, in Mexico, they want to know that the nearby hurricanes are stirring up trouble and that trouble is manifesting itself as mountains of water in the double-overhead range. *Double-overhead* is a shifty term. Technically, it means exactly what it sounds like, that the waves are double the height of an average man or somewhere around ten to twelve feet. Metaphorically, it's the dividing line between business and pleasure.

I ordered a beer from a woman who may very well have been the best-looking bartender in all of Mexico. Things were looking up. I asked one of the other guys in the pool how the surf was.

"Big."

"How big?"

"I mean big."

Things stopped looking up nearly as fast as they started. I was both addicted to surfing and terrified of surfing. The last surf trip I had taken was to Indonesia, and that was seven years back. In Indonesia, I learned one rather simple lesson: how easy it is to drown.

7

In 1996, about four years into my career as a writer, the country of Malaysia decided to put its northernmost province, the island of Penang, online. The plan was to run fiber to every corner and every curb, to hot-wire hospitals, hotels and hovels—the whole damn place really—and somehow I persuaded a magazine to send me to cover it. Because I had never been to that part of the world before, I wanted to extend my stay and look around. Because I was dirt-poor at the time, I called everyone I knew and mentioned I would be over in that part of the world and asked if they happened to need anything. You know, the usual: drink umbrellas, dengue fever, an article, whatever. Another editor from another magazine suggested I check out Komodo Island, and not knowing any better, I agreed. At the time of this suggestion, I had no idea that Komodo was in Indonesia, but after I figured that out I realized I could make some quick cash with a surf story in Bali and then catch a boat to dragon land. There were a few problems with that plan. Uppermost among them was the fact that I hadn't surfed in three years and back when I was surfing I was never much good. But I didn't mention these things to anyone, and one sunny December day in the midnineties I found myself in Bali.

If you've spent some time roaming the edges of the world, you've discovered that there are a lot of other people out there roaming with you. A good portion of these people would rather be anyplace besides where they are or where they came from. Many would rather be in Mecca, whether or not they realize Mecca is a city caught in a sandstorm surrounded by desert surrounded by war. Nearly half of Jamaica wants to be in Ethiopia, never mind that it's not really a country in Africa they desire, but a mystical place somewhere between Marcus Garvey and the gates of heaven. But Bali is a place where people run to and stay forever. It's a dream state, and some of its dreamers never awaken.

At the time I was there, the daily wage hovered just over two dollars, roughly fifty cents of which the locals spent each morning on small religious offerings. The offerings were made of areca nut, betel leaf and lime, red, green and white being the colors of Brahma, Vishnu and Shiva respectively, often augmented with currency and cigarettes—though why any god would want to smoke Indonesian cigarettes remains something of a mystery. The offerings are known as *banten,* which means "gift," or *enten,* which means "consciousness." Either way, one quarter of the typical Balinese below-poverty-line income was spent every day on a tribute to their beliefs.

Some believe in a horny goddess known as Ratu Nyai Loro Kidul, queen of the Southern Seas. Every year she plucks several young men from the nearby ocean to be her lovers. Among her favorite hunting grounds are the water of Nusa Dua. If you ask the locals, they'll tell you that Nusa Dua is the Sunset Beach of Indonesia. If you ask what this means, well maybe they know or maybe they don't. Maybe it's something they heard or read, or maybe they just like the way the words play in their mouths. It might mean that Nusa Dua is a bowling alley on the moon. Or a great spot for a tryst. Or a pristine expanse of white sands and luxury hotels where you can get a good tan and buy expensive mangoes. But to surfers it means only big, serious waves breaking over the sharp teeth of a coral reef on the southern tip of the island of Bali.

I'd been there for three weeks. I'd surfed the beginner waves at Kuta and Legian and paddled out at Canggu, where the waters rise over black lava and the surfers all speak Japanese. I'd hitched a ride on a logging truck west up the coast to Medewi—a slow, fat wave perfect for longboards and an afternoon snooze. I knew enough not to try and paddle out at Padang-Padang. I knew that Padang-Padang was a place to confront mortality. I knew the nearest hospital was a plane ride away in Singapore or Jakarta. I knew that to screw up there was to be very, finally, fucked. But I knew nothing about Nusa Dua—not until I met the Australians.

I met the Australians because I had woken in the middle of the night to find the door to my bungalow jimmied open and a man with a flashlight pawing through my backpack. Despite being completely naked, I leaped up and gave chase. I think it was my passport I was worried about as we dashed across the darkened lawn, past a long line of bungalows and directly into a hedge. On the other side of the hedge there was a six-foot brick wall that separated the hotel from the rest of the city. My burglar vaulted the wall, and I vaulted after him, catching my foot on the way over, ending up sprawled naked in the middle of a very crowded street. Kuta is where half of Australia goes on spring break, and it was spring break and bar time and people were everywhere. None seemed to happy to find me suddenly in their midst, least of all the military police less than twenty feet away.

Before I was even back on my feet, they had started my way and I had started to contemplate exactly what happened when a naked American went to an Indonesian jail. Moments before they arrived, a group of drunken Australians decided, in what I can only assume was a moment of divine inspiration, to block the police's path. They used the traditional techniques—stumbling and swearing the main components. They bought me ten seconds, but it was enough. I jumped back over the wall and dashed to my bungalow and slammed and locked the door and wedged a chair beneath the handle for good measure. As it turns out, my passport was still beneath my pillow, where I'd hidden it hours before, for safekeeping.

The next day, this time fully clothed, I bumped into the same Australians again. I told them the story and bought them some beers to say thanks, and they bought me some beers because they were Australian. Then we made up a few more excuses and kept on drinking. In the end we all had a few too many, and in the process they managed to convince me to go surf Nusa Dua with them the next day.

Hungover and standing on the shore at Nusa Dua, I thought the waves looked like medium-sized curlers, a little fast maybe, yet utterly manageable. But in the boat, drawing near, I got a better look. Nusa Dua is an outer reefbreak. *Reefbreak* is a fancy way of saying lots of rock underwater, and Nusa Dua is an outer reefbreak because the rock sits far offshore, completely exposed to the full brunt of the ocean's power. The wave that results is something of a wondrous monster. On a big day there's no margin for error. Not that the Australians were making any errors. They did all the things good surfers do, catching waves like most people catch buses. I was watching them cut it up and down the line as if they were doing something I didn't understand, something I hadn't put a few years of my life into, something alien and mysterious, like golf.

I caught a wave. It took a while and it wasn't nearly the size of the leviathans my friends were catching, but it came in well overhead and I saw it starting to form in the distance, and before I had time to think things through I spun my board and dug in deep. I heard shouts of "Paddle, motherfucker, paddle" from the Aussies, then I heard nothing but the roar of water. The water that was roaring toward me was quite literally a memory. It started out in some other part of the world, forming when a change in temperature produced a change in pressure. Air's natural tendency is to move from an area of high pressure to an area of low pressure. We call this movement wind. When wind flickers across the ocean's surface, it produces small ripples which provide a greater surface area that can then catch more of that blowing wind. Eventually these ripples become larger and larger until they cohere into wavelets and eventually waves, attaining their greatest size when they come closest to matching the wind's speed. What makes this whole chain of events slightly stranger is that it is not the water itself traveling across the ocean as a wave, but merely the memory of the original wind's energy being constantly transferred as vibration from one neighboring water molecule to the next. When I heard the roar of that wave behind me at Nusa Dua, what I was actually hearing was the sound of the past arriving in the present with me directly in its path.

On the wave I chose, its peak—both its highest point and the first section to break—was fifteen feet to my left. Ideally, you want to paddle into a wave by lining up dead center with that peak, timing things so it arrives right behind you just as the lip's about to pitch. I was fifteen feet away because that pitching lip represents the greatest transfer of energy in this wave's life and getting to one's feet beneath that lip requires the agility to go from horizontal to vertical in the exploding milliseconds it takes for this transfer to happen. Technically, this involves laying hands flat on the front of the board, roughly in line with the shoulders, then pushing down evenly and steadily. You are both pushing yourself up to a standing position and pushing the surfboard down into the ever-steepening wave. Timed just right, feet hit board as board drops into wave. Good surfers do this with the incredible economy of motion required to keep things steady at a point when nothing is steady. Bad surfers fall down a lot.

In the three weeks I had been in Bali I had already fallen down plenty, but falling down at Nusa Dua was not an experience I wanted to have. It was fear that got me to my feet and wax that kept them in one place. Surfers put wax on their boards for traction, and the coat on mine was so thick you could barely see the fiberglass beneath. For added stability, my knees were bent deep and my stance was wide, but this was the biggest wave I had ever been on and nothing could have prepared me for the speed. Blurry, dizzy, warping speed that sent the world flashing by in snatches too quick for my brain to process. I felt like I had fallen off a building and landed atop a greasy express train, and that express train seemed none too pleased to have the company.

Surfer's use the term *bottom turn* to mean both any turn made at the bottom of the wave and more frequently the first such turn made on a wave. A good bottom turn sets up the whole ride, taking all of the energy of the initial drop and turning it into all the momentum needed to climb back up to the crest and fire on down the line. To make this happen, you begin in a low crouch and then whip first head then shoulders then arms in the direction of the wave's face. At the same time, you're straightening legs and rocking slightly backward onto your heels, both powering into the turn and shaping the water beneath the board into the miniature ramp it needs to climb back up. Since I ride goofyfoot, with my right foot forward and my left foot back, I was riding with my back to the wave. This meant the first time I got a real good look at it was also the moment I started my first bottom turn. When I finally saw the size of things, I was not thinking, Oh, look there's a giant memory of wind.

I think the thought was somewhere along the lines of: Holy shit, I better get the hell out of here fast. One of the good things about surfing is that events take place at such high speeds that no sooner did I have this thought than I was already out of the way of that danger and ready for whatever came next. What came next was one of the Aussies paddling back out to the break. He was directly in front of me. I was going to decapitate him if I didn't find a way to turn or he didn't find a way to duck. I swerved and he ducked, and the last thing I saw as he dropped beneath the surface was one lone finger wagging in my direction—a little reminder perhaps of the camaraderie of surfers.

I passed him and rode on until the wave crossed another shallow section of reef and started to rear up and pitch over. I had lost too much speed in my antidecapitation maneuver and was never going to make that next section. Instead I angled my board up the wave's face and flailed off the backside in a kind of ecstatic belly flop. I don't remember paddling back out to the lineup. I know that once there, I did everything I could to contain myself. Shouting "Did you see that? Did you see that? Did you see that?" is generally frowned upon. That said, it should also be pointed out that there is an unspoken dictum in surfing which states "the best surfer in the water is the one having the most fun." And for those few moments, I was definitely the best surfer in the water.

Then, suddenly, possibly adrenaline-drunk with my newfound prowess, I made an error. It didn't seem like one at the time, but errors never do. I paddled into another wave without careful study. Instead of positioning myself a little farther down the line, I lined up directly with the peak. Clearly, my one ride had made me an expert. As the wave reached me I felt the back of the board start to rise and then the rest of the board start to rise, and then I was caught by some terrible aquatic elevator. The wave was enormous. By the time I knew what was happening, the bottom was already dropping out, and when the lip threw, I was not quite at my feet. That was my second error. I didn't get a third.

In the early sixties, a man named Frederick Brown won a magazine contest by writing one of the world's shortest science fiction stories. The story was as follows: "The last man on Earth hears a knock at the door." That was about what I felt like for those long airborne moments before I landed directly beneath what was quickly becoming one of the dumbest things I'd ever done in my life. Almost, but not quite. They say that Ratu Nyai Loro Kidul has a thing for boys in green shorts. All of her lovers wore—and the past tense is important here—green shorts. I'm still not sure if the only reason I'm alive today is that my shorts were black.

After that fall and the pummeling and the raking over the reef and the gasping for oxygen and the whimpering animal sounds, came the next wave and more pummeling and more raking over the reef and more gasping for oxygen and more whimpering animal sounds. After the six or seven waves that followed had all had their turn, I finally made it back to the boat. I was cut up pretty badly. It took me about twenty minutes to stop puking up water. Around the time I did, one of those Aussies paddled over and said something quaint and reassuring like "Close one, mate." I nodded in agreement and bled a little bit more and said something about the goddess of the Southern Seas feeling forgiving this morning. He shook his head no. "That wasn't any goddess; that was just the Conductor having his way with you."

"The who?"

"The Conductor."

"What are you talking about?"

So he told me a story about two guys on an epic surf quest who get lost near the ass-end of nowhere and meet some guy who could control the weather and conduct the waves with some kind of baton made from human bone—it was a pretty curious story— but it went on and on and I was waterlogged and bedraggled and forgot all about it and might never have remembered except that seven years later I took a trip to Mexico and there, too, something went horribly wrong.

8

On my fourth day in Mexico, one of the nearby hurricanes quit threatening and finally swept up the coast. Instead of staying out to sea and producing epic swell, it veered too close to shore and produced epic mess. Trees groaned and creaked and were blown sideways, and the ones that didn't uproot entirely bent far and flung their coconuts across the beach in angry protest. The pool at Costa Azul turned dingy and overflowed, and the excess water formed tributaries and estuaries and miniature malarial swamps. The thatched roof of the Tiki hut leaked. It leaked less than the rest of the world seemed to be leaking, so every stray dog in town showed up for a chance to stay dry under its long eaves. For the surfers who had decided to hang around and risk the storm, there was nothing much to do, so we did what one does in Mexico when there's nothing much to do: watch stray dogs, drink beer.

The morning of the fifth day dawned bleary. The rain had stopped, but the sea was still rough. We were an hour away from the spot where we hoped to surf, and there was no way to check the conditions. A cell phone would have worked wonders, but there were none, and the storm had knocked down power lines so there were no regular phones either. We had no other options. Eight of us piled into a van for the trip to the harbor to see what we could see.

One of the surfers, a lanky New Yorker named Ben, was riding shotgun. Back home, he worked long hours as a day trader of some kind in Manhattan but tried to surf every morning at the Jersey shore. People who surf the Jersey shore always say that there are waves there equal in girth and threat to Hawaii's legendary Pipeline. The normal response to this statement is that whoever is making it has never surfed Pipeline. But Ben had surfed Pipeline, and even if he hadn't, he got up most days before work to ride waves as cold as ice cubes. In the winter he would have to climb through the snowdrifts to get to the water's edge. He seemed tougher than most, unflappable.

As we drove, the windows on the van kept fogging up, and Ben took it upon himself to keep wiping them clean. About ten miles down the road, while he was rubbing a clean spot on the window in front of him, he suddenly shouted, "What the fuck is that?" It was a fair question. About a hundred yards ahead of us someone was driving in a cement mixer backward, at about fifty miles an hour, directly toward us. We swerved, he swerved, and many of us vowed to give up drinking completely.

After the hangover and the cement mixer came the harbor. It wasn't much more than a muddy cul-de-sac at the edge of a muddy town. The air smelled of dead shrimp. As it turns out, the harbor was covered in dead shrimp. It looked like the aftermath of an explosion at a shrimp canning factory. They were everywhere. When we parked and got out, the dead crunched under our feet. The stink, the stink was awful.

When the harbormaster thought the surf too dangerous for fishing boats to risk, he hung a red flag from a flagpole that stood atop a small shack at the water's edge. It's a good bet that someone made a living in that shack peeling shrimp and flying flags. Today the flag was flying red, which meant that the harbor was closed and the ocean too dangerous. We hoped that the harbormaster was in bed, hungover, and the red flag was still hanging from yesterday.

There was little proof of this, but we had come to surf and suffered much and would not be denied.

In *For Whom the Bell Tolls,* Ernest Hemingway said there were two rules for getting on with people who speak Spanish: "give the men your cigarettes and leave the women alone." In dealing with our apprehensive boat captain, we followed both of them and added in about fifty bucks. One out of the three seemed to do the trick.

"Casa de loco" is what he said by way of agreement.

Casa de loco loosely means "the house is crazy." Over the years, I've heard a number of different Spanish-speaking men mutter this phrase, but when I've asked other Spanish-speaking men if it's a common expression they universally shake their heads no. This leads me to believe that somewhere, through those few degrees of separation, all these various phrase-uttering men have a common ancestor of sorts, and that whatever else might be said about this ancestor, one thing is certain: his house was crazy.

Our boat captain didn't care to comment much about the origin of the phrase and instead set about readying the boat. He didn't look too happy, but truthfully it wasn't much of a trip. Twenty minutes away was where we wanted to go, a reef break called Chacala. At every surf destination in the world there are waves that people talk about and waves that people *talk* about. At Costa Azul people *talk* about Chacala.

They talk about catching Chacala big, and that day it was going to be big. "Triple overhead," people said. It was a mantra. It echoed in my head. I had surfed seriously overhead waves no more than twenty times in my life and had surfed real triple overhead once, and that had been at Nusa Dua, an experience I hoped to avoid duplicating. Furthermore, Chacala barrels, and I had never successfully surfed a big barreling wave before. While I was sure I could learn to surf such barrels, I wasn't sure I could do so without falling. Unfortunately, Chacala is not an easy wave to fall from. The wave breaks over a very shallow reef and that reef is covered in sea urchins and those sea urchins are covered in barbed spines. It doesn't take a rocket scientist to figure out that falling at Chacala on a triple-overhead day means nothing good. In our group there were plenty of surfers better than me, and plenty of them had packed first-aid kits in their backpacks that morning.

A few months back a woman had been surfing Chacala on a big day. She duck dove through a wave and once underwater had a brief argument with a bonefish. She ended up with a fish spine stuck into her arm at the bicep and out of her arm through the triceps. This seemed to be exactly the kind of argument that was typical of the spot, but I was in no hurry to find out. My enthusiasm seemed to be shared by the boat captain, who looked at the sky and crossed himself before starting the motor.

Getting to Chacala required punching out of a small bay and following the coastline north. The waves in the bay were roguish and choppy, but once we pushed out into open water the swell seemed to cohere into a pattern that felt a little like riding a mechanical bull: dangerous, but predictable in its violence.

"I think it's going to be big," I said to Ben. He glanced at me and gazed back over the bow at the ragged chop and said, "It's better not to think about it."

Devotees of Tibetan White Lineage Buddhism believe that on the other side of every negative emotion is a positive one. Like hate is the opposite of love and ecstasy the opposite of fear. In this form of Buddhism the idea is to raise the level of one's vibration to change one emotion into the other. While I have no idea what this really means, I do know that during the period of time when I was the sickest, I found that if I went right at the thing I was most afraid of, I usually ended up happier for it. It should be pointed out that during the period of time when I was the sickest, because Lyme has a peculiarly hallucinogenic effect, it was even odds that the thing I was the most afraid of didn't actually exist at all. Either way, I had decided to see where my theory took me. That day it took me to Chacala.

9

The best advice I had ever been given about surfing was given to me a few weeks before I arrived in Mexico. I had gone through a short period of feeling lousy and a longer period of recovery and come out the other end and gone surfing. I was ridiculously rusty and mostly managed some rather spectacular falls. Many of these falls were happening because my timing was off and sections of the waves kept snapping closed before I could dart through them. The guy I was surfing with told me I needed to look where I wanted to go and not where I was going. In other words, don't look at the section of the wave that is about to slam closed on top of you, but look past it to the place where the wave's shoulder is, and usually you will end up there. One of the first things I realized that day at Chacala was the importance of this advice.

Taking off on a wave on big days is not exactly the same as taking off on a small wave on a small day only bigger. On a small day taking off means glancing at the oncoming wave, picking the spot where you want to be when you start taking off, paddling like hell for it and, at the moment when the wave starts to lift, standing up and driving down into it. With a little practice, on a small day, this is fairly easy to do. On a big day things are different.

The main thing that's different is that when you glance at the oncoming wave, it looks about the same size as a house. Most people, when they find themselves directly in the path of a moving house, have an instinctual get-me-the-hell-out-of-here response. If you can ignore that response, you turn around and paddle. The problem with this is that when you paddle into a big wave, if you continue looking at the spot where you're going, you'll notice that spot is now some fifteen feet below you, off the edge of a roiling cliff. Moreover, as things progress and you've crashed over that cliff, you'll notice that that moving house is getting ready to land on top of you. But if you look where you want to go, you'll miss noticing these things and instead notice a wide-open shoulder of the wave. This shoulder is nowhere near as steep as the pit in front of you, and if you can make it there, odds are you can avoid getting killed for a little while longer.

For these reasons, others, most of that morning I avoided being killed. Most of this was luck, but I could have cared less. I was punch-drunk on adrenaline, paddling gleefully into big surf for the first time in my life. I was riding a spitting, swaggering crush of water. *Casa de loco,* baby. And then I made an error. It didn't seem like an error at the time. I had been surfing Chacala for most of the morning. The waves were coming in sets of five, with the fourth being the biggest of the bunch. Because of this, the fourth wave always broke farther outside and didn't just break left but went right as well. The rights were a dicey proposition. They petered out on a nasty pile of rocks, and since there was at least one other wave behind them, if you didn't find a way off those rocks rather quickly, that other wave was going to land on you and mash you onto those rocks. But other guys had been riding them, and I wanted to give it a shot. My error was bravado.

There were a number of things I hadn't counted on about going right. I hadn't counted on the fact that because I was surfing into the rocks, the water was shallower and the wave steeper. And faster. Much faster. And while neither was too much of a problem, the real problem was that the wave I had chosen didn't want to stay open. As soon as I dropped into the wave, I got swallowed by the wave. I got the washing machine. I got mashed onto the rocks. Shit happens. Then more shit happened.

Unlike every other set of the day, this one didn't have five waves; it had—well, I lost count. A better surfer or a smarter surfer would have ripped off his leash and swam in, but by the time I realized this was an option I was out of options. I got mashed onto the rocks. I was running out of breath and bleeding in a couple of places and starting to think that I might drown here when I heard Ben shouting, "Get the hell out of there." It was pretty straightforward advice, but since I had lost my ability to think, having someone else do it for me somehow seemed to make the difference.

Truthfully, I don't know how I got out of the pit. I don't know if there were more waves to paddle through. I don't remember paddling at all. The next thing I knew, I was pretty far outside the break, gasping for air. No bones were broken, though the next morning I found a bruise that started near my hip and ran to my shoulder. But at the time I didn't notice because Ben had paddled over.

"Looks like the Conductor had his way with you" was what he said.

10

It was the same story I had heard in Indonesia. Of course, I didn't recognize it at first. At first, I was just listening to Ben talk about two blokes who chased a surf rumor right off the edge of the world. That was his phrase, how he chose to put it. I often think about following an idea right off the edge of the world. Perhaps that's understandable. From the right angle, all of life is foreshadowing.

One way or another they were two men on a surf quest, and every surfer instinctively understands that rubric. Two-time world champion Tom Carroll wrote of it once, in the foreword to Matt Warshaw's *Surf Riders: In Search of the Perfect Wave*: "From the start, my companions and I saw surfing as an invitation to explore. After we'd covered every inch of our local beach, we'd plan a jaunt around the nearby rocky headland to the next beach over. Maybe there'd be better waves there. And what about the next beach up the headland? We'd find out soon enough."

Surfers always seem to find out soon enough. The quest for the perfect wave has mixed in with the gene code of the sport, fundamental to its DNA. So the Conductor's story starts where such stories start, with two men on the trail of a rumor, hunting what novelist Kem Nunn once called the "premier mysto wave, the last secret spot." Who knows where they went? They certainly went out

37

past the far end of town where the Grickle-grass grows. "Out to middle fucking nowhere, mate," was how my Aussie friend put it.

Of course the car was a mud clunker, rattling with every bump. From the sound of things, there were plenty of bumps. Drunks in the bars, bandits on the roads, reports of worse. They took a left turn somewhere, left the asphalt highways, drove on into the dirt, kept going until there was no longer anywhere to go. The general thinking on the matter seems to be that they got stuck less than a quarter mile from the ocean—a riverbed perhaps, deep alluvial muck—just close enough to hear the roaring thump of the waves. "They had driven for weeks," said Ben. "The secret was right over the next hill." His eyes stayed pinned to the horizon. "Man, that would suck."

The decision was to hike the rest of the way. The day was one of clear skies and bright sunlight. They got out of the car, untied the boards, were all ready to set out. They got ten feet from the car when their luck changed. Ben drew a zigzag in the air and told me a lightning bolt zapped right into the hood of their car, charring it instantly. "I mean—zap—black."

A lightning bolt?

Ben thought I was missing the point; I wasn't yet convinced there was a point.

"The lightning fried their transmission. They're low on supplies, miles from anywhere, neither knows shit about engines—so they do the only thing that makes any sense at the time."

"They go surfing," I said.

"You know this story?"

I was starting to remember. I recalled that when they finally reached the ocean, the waves were gone. A couple football fields offshore was a thin shadow that might mean an outer reef, no way to tell without paddling out, no reason to paddle out. They waited for most of the afternoon; there was no change, not even a ripple.

Just when they were ready to leave—another zap, another lightning strike.

"It hit the reef," said Ben.

"Poof," I said, "instant waves."

It was all coming back. The waves had appeared in the exact spot the lightning had struck. Of course they formed perfect tubes. This was surf porn; in these kinds of stories the tubes are always perfect. So they paddled out for perfection. Caught waves all afternoon, caught waves right up to the point when there were no more waves. "They just stopped," Ben snapped his fingers, "just turned off."

"Pond flat."

"Exactly."

"Absolutely, pond flat, 'cause that happens."

While I hadn't been surfing all that long, I'd been around the ocean long enough to know that swells took hours to arrive, sometimes longer to leave, but that wasn't my principal concern.

"That's when they saw him, right?"

"The old dude?"

"The one who conducts the waves with a baton made from human bone?"

"Yeah," said Ben, "that was when they saw him."

A couple hundred yards beyond them, farther out to sea, was a man sitting on a surfboard. He appeared out of nowhere, out of mist and shadow, more silhouette than substance. In his hand was a long, white bone. The story goes that it was with this baton that he could conduct the waves, control the weather; perhaps he had other abilities, but no one seemed to know the extent of his power.

I didn't think there were people who could summon weather at will, though I had lived in Phoenix for a little while and there met a Hopi Indian who felt otherwise. His name was John Long John, or that was his claim. He wore a Colt .45 in a beaded holster, mentioned that the Hopi called themselves *Hopitu*—"the peaceful people"—later mentioning other things. "I can bring the rain with a dance. Many of us still can, I'm just particularly good at it."

A few beers after that, he told me that the gods who lived in the great cloud formations atop certain sacred mountains were really beings from outer space. "They hide their flying saucers in those clouds." You could tell, he was sure of it, because the clouds never moved. "When you dance for rain, you learn the secrets. Who ever heard of clouds that don't move?"

That pretty much summed up my opinion on the subject, but I was willing to let the whole weather-control issue slide because I was mildly preoccupied with the fact that I was hearing this story a second time—under some strikingly similar circumstances. I told Ben about the first time, when I was raked over the reef at Nusa Dua. My Aussie friend had called the phantom surfer the Conductor because he could conduct the waves. Ben was sure it was the same story.

Still, we had slightly different versions of what happened next. I remembered that they tried to paddle out to the Conductor right then; Ben said it took place a few days later. It didn't matter. The results were the same. They could never get there. Ten minutes, twenty minutes, they paddled farther and farther out into the ocean, but the Conductor just seemed to drift away. It was the same the next day, the day after. He was always there, but every time they tried to reach him, he was always drifting away.

That wasn't the only magic in the story. In fact, from this point on, the story was almost all magic. In the days ahead, as their supplies dwindled and their situation grew more dire, one of the men tried to hike out for help, but a sandstorm blocked his passage. He came back and tried again and got the same result. Out in the ocean, the Conductor put on the kind of meteorological displays worthy of Poseidon. Waves that appeared from flat water, waves that disappeared as quickly as they had come. Rights and lefts at his command. Storm clouds and lightning and clear skies and no wind and, most important, every time they paddled out—perfect surf.

On the night they ran out of food, the Conductor paid a visit. He emerged out of the darkness, stopping just outside their campsite. Neither could get a good look at him, not even when he came closer. He didn't say much, just went to work under the car's hood, worked without light. Hours passed. Sometime in the middle of that night the engine coughed and sputtered and came to life. Afterward, he reached into his satchel and lifted out the bone and set it on the ground between them. Then he bent down and picked up a bit of loose soil, letting it drift, watching for the direction of the wind. That was the direction he went. He strode off into the desert night, leaving the bone, leaving them almost as he had found them—with the bones of the past, with nothing but the future to look forward to. The next day, when the new sun rose, one of these two men became the new surfer sitting out by the horizon. The other was left on the beach.

Or that's how I heard it, but who the hell knows? Maybe I heard wrong. Ben thought the details unimportant. He was sure it was a myth. I don't recall what my Aussie friend had thought. My own feeling was urban legend, a chunk of pop-culture flotsam, far too modern for a myth.

"Do you know the story of Percival?" Ben asked.

It was then that I felt a dull throb near my ankle. I lifted my leg out of the water and found a deep cut running down my shin. I had been bleeding into the ocean this whole time. It was a fear of sharks that kept me from hearing about Percival right then. I paddled back to the boat; Ben paddled back to the break. He left later that day, going either to New York or deeper into Central America; he didn't want to make up his mind until he got to the airport. It wasn't until I got back home that my friend Joshua reminded me that Percival was the only one of King Arthur's legendary knights to actually find the Holy Grail—though he did so accidentally, merely stumbling upon it on a day he was out looking for other things—which is pretty much how things went with those two surfers and the Conductor.

"You know," said Joshua, "in every successful quest there are mystical prerequisite conditions. Percival might have been the schmuck of the round table, but he was the only one who got to see the Grail because he was the only one whose heart was pure."

I wondered what those conditions were in the Conductor's story, and Joshua started laughing.

"What?" I asked.

"I think the prerequisites were that those guys were surfers and they went looking."

It was sometime later that I learned of the first group of Californian surfers who went to Hawaii for a shot at really big waves. They lived in an army-built Quonset hut on the beach in the town of Makaha. In Hawaiian slang these guys were known as *hellman,* as anyone who consistently braves the winter waves at Waimea is known. But these guys put a big circular table in the center of their living room and took to calling themselves "Knights of the Round Table."

PART TWO

You have lost your camel, my friend
And all around you people are full of advice
You don't know where your camel is,
But you do know that these casual directions are wrong.

—Rumi

11

Mine was not a surfer's childhood. No white sand beaches, no bikini girls. I was raised in the fly-over flats, far from the ocean. Born in Chicago, bred in Cleveland, my earliest aquatic memories belong to bodies of water angling for Superfund dollars. Half a century of big steel and bad decisions had turned Lake Erie into a cesspool of neglect. As kids, we didn't fear its strong currents so much as its strong chemicals. And Erie didn't hold a candle to the Cuyahoga, a river that spent my youth catching fire on more than one occasion. If these waters were sacred to anyone I knew, they never mentioned it.

Mine was a childhood bereft of wet reverences, or reverences of any kind really. My grandparents had traded a past they wanted to forget for a future they could barely imagine. They were immigrants, eastern European Jews, but the faith they had carried across that ocean had more to do with survival than spirituality, and that was an attitude I didn't come to understand until much later. Even the traditions passed down—the two sets of dishes, the Shabbos blessings, the lighting of the menorah—had the feel of something lost in someone else's dusty closet. These were the things that Jews did; no one seemed to remember why.

My earliest childhood belief, if that phrase is even apt, was the sneaking suspicion that the world was a much more mysterious place than people were letting on. It's hard to say how much of this was suburban boredom and how much heartfelt sentiment, and in the end it didn't matter. I wanted out and more and different and, around the time I turned eleven, discovered these things at the local magic store: Pandora's Box, located on the second tier of Richmond Mall, kitty-corner to the pet store, near the bench where the girls in tube tops liked to sit and smoke cigarettes.

There's a certain straightforward logic at work here. A child who believed that there were deeper mysteries went looking for them at the local magic store, but the truth was that Pandora's Box was the first place I remember feeling safe. Professional prestidigitators are a weird lot; apparently I fit in just fine. Even when I didn't, no one, not once, ever asked me to leave. So I stayed. For two years, for three years, for five, my days were spent absorbing card tricks, coin tricks, all sorts of other things.

There was a woman named Lorelei, a redheaded beauty, who worked part-time at the shop and part-time as a tarot reader and part-time as a go-go dancer. When we met, I was in sixth grade and having a hard time of it. I was a skinny kid, not much of a pugilist. There were lots of fights; I lost most. Lorelei sat me down one day, after noticing the set of bruises dotting my arm. "The pendulum always swings both ways," she told me, and backed it up with a mishmash of physics and phenomena, part karma, part relativity, but she could have used toothpaste and Pink Floyd lyrics, for all I cared. Here was an adult telling me that there were other forces at work, things out of sight, things incomprehensible. She reinforced what I already suspected, and by the time I was out of high school, that lesson had grown into a full-blown metaphysics. In hindsight, it might have just been a bad case of *Jonathan Livingston Seagull*-itis, but it felt so much bigger back then.

High school gave way to college, but I hadn't lost my lust for mystery. There were plenty of classes in psychology and philosophy and religion—really anything that smacked of forbidden knowledge and deeper secrets—though none of it seemed to deliver. After four semesters of this, I decided the things I needed to learn weren't to be found in academia, instead dropping out of school to move to Santa Fe, New Mexico, because the New Age was booming. This was the rabbit hole all right; the whole town seemed permanently strung out on mescaline. I had arranged to spend my first few nights there with the cousin of a friend of a friend or some other infinite regress of I don't know who the hell you are, but who am I to argue with a free bed? His name was Paul. On the way back from the airport Paul told me that occasionally there was some trouble with aliens. He was so calm about the whole thing, I thought he was talking about illegal immigrants. Apparently, he meant the other kind—the kind that travel in flying saucers. He claimed they talked to him, asked him to do things; occasionally there were disagreements.

"So if you hear some shouting later tonight, just ignore it."

"Uh-huh," I said. "Anything else I should know?"

"Well, tonight being Saturday, you should probably stay away from the windows."

"'Cause of the aliens?"

He shook his head.

"Aliens don't bother with windows."

Bullets were the problem with the windows. My host lived at the bottom of a deep ravine. On the top of the left side of the ravine lived one of the local drug lords, and on top of the right side lived another of the local drug lords. Five hundred feet separated their respective compounds, with Paul's house smack in the middle. "This being Saturday and all," Paul said, "they can get pretty drunk and start shooting at one another."

I don't know about the aliens, but he wasn't kidding about the drug lords. The gunfire lasted all night; in the morning I found another place to live. Did it get better? It certainly got something. In the coming months I learned to throw the *I Ching*; I fell in love with a woman who ran a crystal store. In a back room of that crystal store was a giant copper pyramid. I spent hours inside that pyramid, learning to meditate with amethyst crystals taped above my third eye. Past-life regressions, astral projection, the profound effects of Mercury going retrograde, the dangers of working with black obsidian energy, the healing power of colon therapy—these were frequent topics of conversation. I worked as a waiter and frequently got tipped in hallucinogens, ten hits of acid the going rate for good service. Because I lived in a bad part of town, when I had to stay late at the restaurant, a pair of armed Mexicans occasionally walked me home. These men were not affiliated with the eatery but were my escorts through the deep barrio because I had accidentally befriended the local warlock. I won't tell you about the things that warlock did with chickens.

When I think back on my time in New Mexico, one night stands out clearer than most. A legendary South American shaman had come through town, and my girlfriend decided what I needed most was a one-on-one soul-healing session with the man. His usual fee for such work was seven hundred dollars, but he had had a past relationship with the crystal store and as a favor agreed to waive it in my case. So I arrived at a small cottage in the hills and was greeted by the tallest man I had ever seen in real life, extremely pale, skinny as a rail, dressed in beige trousers, a purple and green plaid golf shirt and a gargantuan necklace carved from human bone. I was stripped naked and laid out on a long table. Every inch of my body was covered with over a half ton of medicine blankets, eagle feathers, owl claws, tree bark, sacred river stones, sacred mountain stones, crystals of all sizes, power objects of all sorts including a petrified raccoon penis. Lights were shut off, candles lit, the thermostat felt pegged over a hundred. Two women walked into the room. They had come to perform psychic energy work, were of indeterminate age, dressed head-to-toe in white cotton. Performing psychic energy work seemed to involve standing about five feet back from the table and wiggling their fingers in my general direction. A Peruvian Indian in a black loincloth showed up next. Peruvian Indians are generally diminutive in stature. Standing next to the shaman, this guy looked like a dwarf. The dwarf sat down in a corner and pulled out a set of tribal drums and began to beat his fingers raw. The shaman himself towered above me, chanting in a language I had never heard before, his eyes rolled so far back into his head that only the whites were visible. It was too hot, too strange; the drumming was getting louder; the chanting was getting louder; the finger wiggling was verging on semaphore. I was starting to feel like my sacred soul-healing session was being scripted by David Lynch. Then I started to lose consciousness. I had one last thought before I passed out: what if my mother could see me now?

If I had a lick of common sense, it would have ended there—but it didn't. In the coming years, there were ashrams, monasteries, strange teas, strange mushrooms, Sanskrit chants, Native American medicine men with headdresses made from whole otters, folks on the run from the law, folks on the run from much worse. I signed on for the full tour. It lasted for years. By the time I made it back to college, I could sit in the full lotus for six hours at a time, but that was about it. I never, not once, achieved a mystical anything.

It wasn't that I needed all that much, simply proof of concept. I wanted something, anything really, that felt like a spiritual experience. Not that I had any idea what a spiritual experience was supposed to feel like, but I was pretty certain this was the kind of thing I would recognize when it happened. It never happened. Over the course of the next ten years, I lost interest. I still hoped that there was a place where exalted magics were possible, but I no longer lived in that part of the world. Since I didn't go in for the big-invisible-man-in-the-sky theory, there wasn't a whole lot left. Life wasn't that mysterious after all. Then I got good and sick and stayed in bed for years and might have been there still, but one fine spring day a friend called and asked if I wanted to go surfing—and that's when things got a little peculiar.

12

On the day he called I wasn't thrilled about getting back in the ocean. It had been six years since I'd been on a board and had no serious plans of returning. Even if you ignore my last surf experience—the near drowning in Bali—the sport had never been much fun for me. I'd learned to surf in San Francisco, where the water's cold and the waves serious. At Ocean Beach, just paddling out often felt like a life-threatening experience. I remember days when I never even made it to the lineup, forget about catching a ride. The rides there were often short, often mean, the currents treacherous. After a few years of little progress, I stopped trying. Some of this was frustration; most was memory.

The memory was of Chris Marchetti, the man who had taught me to surf. At the time of my instruction, Chris was twenty-three years old and given to unusual methods. "Show it to me, mother-fucker," was often the extent of his surfing advise. Out of habit he liked to holler such advice. A few years prior, he'd been the coxswain on the famed University of Wisconsin crew team. That team had forty-eight trophies in its glass case, including the 1990 National Championship won with Chris shouting them on. He always liked a good shout. When the ocean would flatten between sets, Chris liked to scream "Bring it on" at the horizon. Even if you're not superstitious, you don't scream at something that covers three quarters of the planet. Chris just didn't care. It was often frightening, the way he loved to paddle into waves far beyond his abilities, gleefully seeking out the worst wipeouts imaginable. He said he wanted to see what would kill him. In the end, it wasn't the waves that got that chance.

Chris was cut off while riding his motorcycle in the half-light of the early morning one Easter Sunday. He laid twenty-five feet of skid marks across that San Francisco intersection and then laid his head into the side of a bright yellow tow truck. He never left the bike; his hand still gripped the throttle. His neck had snapped on impact. For weeks afterward his friends would say that when he saw what was coming, he lowered his head, gunned that throttle and screamed "Bring it on."

After Chris died, for most who knew him, surfing was just never the same. I would occasionally give it a go, but it never felt right. My trip to Bali was the very last of those occasions. Years passed; I moved on to other activities, Lyme among them. It took the doctors a very long while to figure out what was wrong with me. Much of that time I spent thinking about Chris's last few seconds on the planet, thinking about what it meant to shout at the inevitable. The day that my friend called to invite me to go surfing was a day near the tail end of my second year with the disease. I had already lost twenty-five pounds, had already lost much more. My doctors had told me there was no way to know if I was strong enough to do anything unless I tried to do something. They claimed I wasn't going to get any sicker, or not in a permanent fashion, but that wasn't saying much. Truthfully, I went surfing because I was already done. My ass had been kicked but good. Illness had won. I could no longer write; I could barely walk across a room. Long ago I had decided that given the right set of impossible circumstances, calling it quits was always an option. I went surfing because I had been contemplating suicide for months and decided I could try one more detour before heading down that route. I went because that's what Chris would have done.

My friend took me to Sunset Beach. Unlike its Hawaiian namesake, California's version is a beginner's wave predominantly peopled by geriatrics, the unskilled, the terrified. Most learn there and never go back. The waves are too soft and too slow, and on the day we went there was no swell in sight. The surf was barely two feet high, but the water was warm and the tide low and I could almost wade to the lineup. I sat out there for about thirty seconds before a wave came. Because it was a crap day at a crap break, there were no other takers. I spun my board around, paddled twice and was on it. For the first time in nearly two years, and just for one wave-riding instant, I felt the thrum of life, the possibility of possibility, and maybe that was enough.

I don't remember anything else about that ride, except that when it was over I wanted another and another and another. Five waves later I wasn't just exhausted; I was disassembled. Those five waves took me fifteen days in bed to recover from, but on the sixteenth I drove back for more. The waves were still small; the water was still warm. I caught five more waves and again spent another two weeks recovering. But I kept coming back, and slowly, very slowly, I started to feel better. At a time when everything else was gone, when nothing made sense and nothing worked, when suicide seemed a damn viable option, surfing saved my life—and I wanted to know why.

13

The surf-cure was, after all, more than a little ridiculous. Not only was surfing not found among the remedies—common or otherwise—for chronic autoimmune conditions, I wasn't actually doing all that much surfing. In the eighteen-month stretch between the time I got back on a surfboard again and the time I went to Mexico, I was averaging about two trips to the ocean a week. Because I was still incredibly sick through much of this period, my average session consisted of about five waves. Since a typical wave lasts about five seconds, a typical session produced about twenty-five seconds of actual wave-riding time. In the time during which surfing was saving my life, I totaled a little over an hour of actual surfing. That's the math, but from where I was sitting the math didn't make much sense.

Or it didn't make much logical sense, yet there was something else going on that was a little harder to explain. So much of life seemed about trying to find ways to live, but surfing seemed the real deal. It felt like voodoo sport, a homecoming to terra incognita, as surreal and beguiling a feeling as any I had known. I had investigated just about every mystical system known to man and had never found much that satisfied, but when I started riding a big chunk of plastic across a bigger chunk of water, suddenly it was like being given a day pass to an Egyptian mystery school.

When things stopped making logical sense, I became a little concerned. Lyme often induces semischizophrenic delusions. I had

done some pretty crazy things while ill and had come away somewhat uncertain with the veracity of my reality. To suddenly find
myself believing in surfing as if it were about to reveal the secrets
of the Zapruder film seemed not only slightly arbitrary but also seriously retarded. Certainly, I wasn't the first person to feel this way.
The history of wave riding is littered with the detritus of similar
spiritualities, but wasn't I smarter than that, or saner than that, or
some other combination thereof? In this, as in so much else, it
turned out I was wrong.

I had always felt that at their core, spiritual beliefs are a strategy
for getting from point A to point B when there's no discernible
path between such places. Siddhartha was unhappy with his life.
Moses was unhappy with the logic of the universe. Jesus was unhappy with the direction humankind was traveling. Each of these
men devised a way out, a way forward, a way. We call their paths religions, but that's just a fancy way of describing our decision to
move in someone else's general direction—following in the footsteps is the common refrain. Was I just following in the footsteps of
surfers who, needing a way to justify their obsession, had draped it
in a hodgepodge of mystical possibility? Was there really something
magical about wave riding that legitimized my belief? For that
matter, how does the mechanism of belief work anyhow? Why did
I start to believe in surfing? Why does anyone start to believe in
anything? How does belief work, in the body, the mind, our culture, human history?

These were some pretty big questions. I didn't know if I could
even begin to answer them, but I did know that they were heavy
on my mind around the time I went to Mexico. It was into this
mental mix that the Conductor's tale got dumped. It was a story
full of myth and magic. It was a story that had found its way to me
twice in seven years, in two different countries, in two different
parts of the world. Whatever else was true, this was certainly one

well-traveled tale. A fact that seemed to indicate that there was something about this story that plenty of other people found interesting enough to bother remembering and retelling. My sneaking suspicion was they decided to bother because retelling it was a way of expressing an inner truth that might not be so well received in our outer world. I didn't know for sure, but the longer I thought about it, the more I wanted to find out. I kept thinking about it plenty.

When I came back from Mexico with the story stuck in my head, I called Jim White at his home in Pensacola, Florida, to talk it through. I did this because Jim was the kind of person you called with an oddball surf question, or any oddball question for that matter. We had first met in September of 1997, when I was writing a music column about him for *GQ*. On the day we met, Jim drove to the airport to pick me up. When I got off the plane, he was leaning against a pillar in the waiting area, wearing a battered cowboy hat and battered cowboy boots and battered cowboy jeans. "I don't normally dress like this," he said by way of a greeting. "My record label thought I should look the part."

Throughout the years, Jim had dressed for plenty of parts. Decades before this, he had been another man, a man born in San Diego in 1957 and named Mike Pratt. Beneath the weight of that moniker he moved from California to Florida and lived out a life as drug partaker and a drug purveyor and a young surfer with some talent and then a professional surfer of some regard. Soon after, he converted himself into a Pentecostal Christian and abandoned the drugs, but not the waves, and became what would soon become a commonplace combination but at the time was a fairly radical departure from the way these things worked: a surfer for Jesus.

He did all of this before he was twenty-five. Then he suffered a crisis of faith and abandoned surf and church and in 1980 accepted an invitation from his well-connected sister to come live in

New York City and try his hand at modeling. Now, as a devout surfer for Jesus, he had lived in fear of vanity so had not looked into a mirror for almost a decade. "After that," Jim once told me, "the act of trying to become a fashion model in New York was a lot like trying to become an elf."

Nonetheless, he was successful. Appearing in handfuls of glossy magazines, he traveled Europe and dated those pretty girls and, along the way, discovered an innate virtuoso talent for the guitar. He'd never really taken a lesson, but he was a natural. People who heard him decided he should quit modeling and move back to the States and become a musician, and so he did. In 1984 he was busy starving and shopping his demo tape and took a job doing construction, and on the first day of work, through the divine agency of a band saw, he nearly lost three fingers on his fretting hand. His guitar dreams went out the window.

So there was convalescence and film school and a magical love affair gone bad and a mysterious illness that sent him back to Florida to recuperate. While there, he picked up the guitar again and retaught himself to play. The virtuoso talent was gone; in its place came a shifting progression of ghost chords and gothic tales that eventually made their way onto an album called *Wrong-Eyed Jesus*. So I heard the album and got on a plane and flew to Florida to see what was what, and not three days later, at roughly the same moment the aptly named Hurricane Earl struck the Gulf coast, Jim and I decided to go surfing.

We piled in his van and drove. There was an endless line of cars on the road, all heading the other direction, all heading toward dry towels and high ground. We drove through the kind of gale-force bluster that only Earl could muster, not stopping until we reached a now-deserted beach on the now-deserted coast of Alabama. The rain was driving down and the ocean was more soup then swell, but we paddled out beside an old pier where the water was swatting the pylons and tumbling forward in a slightly workable left if your definition of a slightly workable left had been provided by a blind man. So odd was our decision to surf that a photographer from a local paper showed up and snapped photos, and one of those photos ran on the front page the following morning, and everybody who had been too dumb not to head for higher ground tapped their paper and said, "See, it's like I've been telling you, we're really not the dumbest people in Alabama."

Because this is how things usually go in Jim's life and because he is the purest storyteller I have ever known, our Alabama surf story is but one out of millions. Stacked among his mind's collection are hundreds of similar tales, both from his years as a professional wave rider and from the years since he retired. Obviously, I called and asked about the Conductor.

"Well, Special K," he said when I was done. Special K was what Jim called me, as in "Well, Special K, that's something of an unusual story."

"Have you ever heard it or anything like it?"

"I tell you what's so unusual about it. Surfers, as a rule, don't have the world's greatest imaginations."

Which is also true, but strangely counterintuitive, and I said as much.

"Did you know that when the first Christian missionaries got to Hawaii, they tried to ban surfing?"

I didn't.

"They failed. Surfing was more important to them than the threat of eternal damnation. But here's the thing, give or take a few fabled waves, that's just about the only mythological surf story I know."

There was a long pause. I took a sip of coffee from a mug Jim had sent me as a birthday present a number of years ago. The mug was small and brown and looked a lot like a Denny's mug except it had been further sculpted into an exact replica of Saddam Hussein's head, with the coffee sitting in the spot where his brains might have gone.

"What year did you first hear the Conductor story?" he asked finally.

"Nineteen ninety-six."

"That Christian surf ban I just mentioned took place at the end of the nineteenth century. To the best of my knowledge, the Conductor's the first pure mythological surf story to come along in a hundred years."

"Uh-huh."

"You should look into that."

"Yeah," I said, "I was thinking the exact same thing."

"Where you gonna look?"

I hadn't really thought this through. I had no idea where to look, and I said as much.

Jim said, "Did you know in the last Australian census seventy thousand people listed their religion as Jedi?"

"I didn't."

"Do you believe a surfer can control the weather?"

I thought about his question for a little while. It was not that I believed that somewhere out there was a surfer who had, through either happenstance or hard work, learned to control the weather. But I had decided a long time ago that the universe is a place considerably bigger than my imagination and I shouldn't rush to judgment until I had all the facts. Though, since the universe was bigger than my imagination, I would never have all the facts. Basically, I told him, I tried to keep an open mind.

"Beliefs are like stew," he said. "Pinch of this, pinch of that, pretty soon you're really cooking."

14

I hung up the phone with Jim and felt better. I felt like something significant had been cleared up, though I was not yet privy to what. I felt wide awake. It felt unusual. Not nearly as unusual as the conversation that took place later that night while having dinner with a friend. Sometime between the hot and sour soup and the kung pao shrimp I found myself telling him that I was going to try and find out everything I could about the Conductor.

"I know it's borderline," I said, "but I think that's exactly what I'm going to do."

"You mean borderline idiotic?"

"Absolutely," I said. "It might not have a purpose. It might not have a meaning. But I'm out of ideas and this one sounds like fun. Absolutely borderline idiotic."

So I called every surfer I knew and asked them about the Conductor. When that didn't work, I started calling editors at surfing magazines and historians at surf museums and anyone else I could think of who might be able to help. While I never once implied that the story was true, more than a few people took the time to explain all the meteorological reasons why a surfer can't actually control the weather—apparently not even with a baton carved from human bone—but no one had ever heard the story.

It was curious, sure, and more than a little frustrating. The frustration was compounded by the fact that Mexico had worn me out and I was still too weak to do much of anything but sit around the house and make more phone calls to more people who knew nothing about the things I wanted to know. In the middle of all of this my neighbor knocked on my door to ask if I felt strong enough to go surfing. I didn't know, but I didn't know anything else either, so we went to Zeroes.

Zeroes sits on lonely beach off a mostly forgotten stretch of highway near the far northern edge of Los Angeles County. From the water the view is expansive: a long sandy beach, a windbreak of scrub brush, a smattering of tall desert pine and, beyond, the dusty rise of the Santa Monica Mountains. Prehistoric artifacts have turned up in eight different sites within a half mile of this spot. Eight thousand years ago people were living here for the view.

We changed into our wetsuits and hiked down to the water. The waves were head high, dark blue with cold. Bank Wright, in his book *Surfing California,* describes the ride as "vertical drops with piping tubes. Ends in backbreaking shorebreak." He leaves out the part about the tiny take-off spot and the competitive crowds, but that day we got lucky. There had been waves in the water for almost a week and everyone already had their fill. We were the only ones out.

I was riding a shortboard, my first, and one I had ridden only a handful of times. The main difference between riding a longboard and a shortboard is speed. Smaller boards make for less planing surface, so catching a wave on a shortboard requires taking off later. This leaves less time to get to your feet and less time to make it into the wave, but when you do make it into the wave—because less surface area also means less drag—it feels a bit like being shot out of a cannon. Which can take some getting used to.

My neighbor had been a sponsored rider back East, and no sooner did we reach the lineup than I understood why. On a wave that looked certain to be a closeout, he took off late and was swallowed beneath the peak. A second later a deep whoop echoed up out of the water, and a moment after that he reappeared farther down the coast. On a wave that appeared to offer nothing, he got a fifty-foot tube ride.

Waves form tubes when the lip of the wave arcs deep into the trough, creating an open cavity beneath it. In moments of private and pure ecstasy, the lucky surfer can ride in this hollow. Lucky because very few waves tube and waves that do tube do not do it all the time. There are thousands and thousands of variables that can affect a breaking wave, and all of them have to work together to produce a good barrel. Sandbars have to be perfect. Winds have to be amenable. The storms that generate the swell must be powerful enough to generate waves with enough force to tube. The swell direction must line up exactly with the contours of the break's bottom. The water level has to be right, so the tides have to be right, so the moon has to be right. Even then, great barrel rides last six, seven seconds. A ten-second tube ride rivals a walk on the moon.

Pulling into any tube remains among the hardest things to do in surfing. It's considered the ultimate elusive experience, and in watching my neighbor catch that tube I realized that the reason I had not had this experience before was not, as I had supposed, that I had never ridden barreling waves before; it was that I had not realized the waves that I had seen barreling were actually rideable. It was as if I had been staring at a jigsaw puzzle for years, looking for the right piece to complete the picture, only to finally realize it had been in my hand all along.

Not that any of this easily translated into success. I went over the falls five or six times in rapid succession, and then, after finally managing to catch one, I tried to turn too quickly, whipping my torso around before my feet had gotten set, thus spinning myself completely off the board and catching the wave's lip like a hard slap on my cheek. The water was shallow. I bounced off the bottom more than once.

"You need to open your shoulder more to the wave" was the advice I was given.

"I'm trying."

"There is no try; there is only do or don't do" came my neighbor's *Star Wars* rejoinder.

In the last Australian census as it turns out, over seventy thousand people had listed their religion as Jedi. While this seems like a joke to most, I've met plenty, myself included, who when asked if they believe in God or, more specifically, what kind of God they believe in, are apt to answer, "Something like the Force in *Star Wars*." Jack Sorenson, the president of LucasArts, once told the *New Yorker*: "*Star Wars* is the mythology of the nonsectarian world. It describes how people want to live." A quick Internet search of those who want to live this way produces Jedi devotees from almost every country on Earth. Most of these devotees do not believe that George Lucas was a prophet, but merely a man who set down in one place what many people had been thinking for quite a while, which seems to be how things go with most prophets.

Much of Jedi thought is an updated version of Taoism, a religion that dates back to the sixth century BC and is possibly the sole conception of the scholar Lao-tzu, but more likely a consortium of ideas by a variety of thinkers whose work was then summarized by Lao-tzu. Either way, the *Tao-te-Ching* is full of Yoda-esque sayings: *be still like a mountain and flow like a great river.* Alan Watts, the great Western Taoist, whose work became incredibly popular during those *Star Wars* seventies, inadvertently defined the Force while defining the Tao in his *The Watercourse Way* as "the first-cause of the universe. It is a *force* that flows through all life."

But Lucas took things further, adding a good-versus-evil paradigm that Western audiences found fundamentally familiar. The dark side as evil; Darth as Satan. It's an idea most people think of as Judeo-Christian, but really one that goes a bit farther back. In *The Historical Figure of Jesus,* E. P. Sanders, a theologian and professor of religion at Duke University and one of the better scholars on the subject, writes:

> It was apparently during the Babylonian exile (around 550 BCE) that Jews began to be complete monotheists. Previously, they had thought their god was the best god, but they had not denied the existence of other gods. A religion that believes there is only one god has a difficult time explaining evil. Did the one good God create it? Why does he permit it? Faced with the actual existence of both good and evil, some religious traditions have posited the existence of two opposing gods. This is the most distinctive theological belief in Zoroastrianism, which began in Persia in the sixth or fifth century BCE and which influenced Mediterranean thought in several ways. Judaism probably owes to Zoroastrianism the idea that an evil power opposed God. (Christianity, in turn, inherited the idea from Judaism.) Judaism remained true to monotheism and did not grant that there was an opposing god, but it accepted some aspects of the Persian dualism, such as the conflict between God and the forces of evil.

So in understanding "there is no try; there is only do or don't do," I'm understanding an amalgamation of spiritual ideas dating back some three thousand years, which goes a long way toward explaining why seventy thousand people in Australia listed Jedi as their religion. It also shed some light on what Jim White meant by "beliefs are like stew" and gave me a way to backtrack the Conductor's story. And, perhaps stranger still, not thirty seconds after I had been told to do or don't do, I did.

I don't remember much about the wave. I remember seeing the bulge begin to rise and thinking that I was lined up about twenty feet off the peak. I took seven or eight sideways strokes and then straightened out. My board caught hold, and three more deep paddles pulled me into it. Already the offshore winds were whipping spray off the face. I couldn't see. Sometime, during this invisible second of watery blindness, I got to my feet and made my first turn. The wave jacked in an instant. Pumping a surfboard means keeping the weight on the back foot steady while picking up the front foot and slamming it back down again, an action that drives more water across the board's fins and increases acceleration. I only had time to pump my board once when I found myself looking down the wave's swirling, kaleidoscope eye. Somehow my feet were in the right place. I bent my back leg in and dropped toward one knee, reaching out to grab the outside rail. The light vanished, and the world turned turquoise. This was the green room. The barrel. I shot out the other side. In and out and done. My first Jedi tube ride.

15

I moved on to calling folklorists, mythologists, urban mythologists, psychologists, parapsychologists, the Jungians, the Joseph Campbell Society, but nobody had heard of the Conductor. I had heard about him twice in seven years, on two different continents, from two different people. Finding no one who had heard anything close was more than a little disconcerting. I had assumed that for the story to circumnavigate the globe required a network of intermediaries, people who shared enough of a fascination with the tale that they'd at least want to repeat it once or twice, and that some of those who heard this repetition would themselves further the process. Not finding anyone who had done such a thing just didn't make all that much sense. The standard dictionary definition of *coincidence* is "a sequence of events that although accidental seems to have been planned or arranged." Perhaps I had moved beyond the realm of standard definitions. Perhaps I needed a different approach.

If I couldn't track down the story itself, there was a chance that I could backtrack its individual parts in such a way that they would begin to shed light on the collective whole. I decided to take the core components of the Conductor's story—the surf quest, that hint of Eastern mysticism, weather and wave control, that flavor of tropical mythology—and see if I could find a moment in time when outside factors would force all of these parts to intersect and overlap. If I couldn't find the story's moment of physical origin, possibly I could trace the preexisting conditions that conspired to create that moment of physical origin. Maybe, I thought, that would be enough.

So if the Conductor's story began with a surf trip, when did this surf trip take place? It's impossible to know for sure, but it's a good bet that it followed the 1964 release of Bruce Brown's classic *The Endless Summer*. Surfers, coming out of the fifties and on into the sixties, had earned a reputation as beatnik beach bums who were going nowhere fast, and certainly not around the world in search of waves. Before *Endless Summer,* outside of the occasional trip to Hawaii, the surf travel industry was nonexistent. Brown changed all of that, turning the wave safari into a rite of passage as essential to the sport as a good bottom turn.

"Bruce Brown, Robert August, and Mike Hyson found perfect surf at Cape St. Francis, South Africa, in late November 1963," wrote one of surfing's premier anthropologists, Matt Warshaw, in his book *Surf Riders: In Search of the Perfect Wave,* "and the discovery, as presented in Bruce Brown's film *The Endless Summer,* is as much a part of surfing history and lore as a story from the Old Testament." Described in the film, the trio hiked a small desert of sand dunes to come upon what is essentially surf pornography: Seventy-degree water, prevailing offshore winds and perfect waves that Brown tells us exist three hundred days a year, and on some of those days, when the waves are big, a seven-mile ride is possible.

Oddly, while the waves in the film were actually found at Cape St. Francis, very little else in the sequence was real. Brown, though only twenty-six at the time he shot *The Endless Summer,* was already a veteran, and he knew that a little fiction never hurt a good surf story. He staked a precious fifty thousand dollars—the sum total of the profits of his previous four films and every last cent he could borrow—on this film. He knew his career hung in the balance. So, as Warshaw points out, he faked it.

Setting the factual record straight, the prevailing wind at Cape St. Francis is not offshore, and a surfer would be more likely to see a troupe of hula dancers gyrate across the Cape than a set of 15-foot waves peeling off for 7 miles. Brown's 300-good-surf-days-a-year claim was overstated by about 285 days. He relied on an even higher degree of poetic license to create the dune-filled "discovery" sequence . . . It might be said that the entire *Endless Summer* project was born in deception starting with the title. Brown knew that the best waves are found in winter, not summer. But he also knew that Midwesterners would never drive through sleet and snow to see a movie called *The Endless Winter.*

In other words, the myth that begat a myth was itself a myth. But that did little to change the film's ripple effect. Within a few years of its release, taking advantage of the burgeoning international transportation industry, wave riders began pushing into all sorts of forgotten corners. In 1996, when I went to Bali for the first time, I made a point of visiting the Uluwatu Temple, where I fed peanuts to monkeys and found a monk who pointed out the spot where the surf photographer Alby Falzon glanced out a window in 1972. On the other side of that window was a jungle that fed into a ravine that poured into a cave that opened onto a reef that formed what *Surfer* magazine recently called "the daddy of all dream waves." The monk summed it up best when he said, "Here they stood, here they saw."

Uluwatu, as the wave has come to be known, was a clarion call to all those wanting to get out and go far. It was among the first in a series of dream discoveries that helped define the modern era of surfing. A few months later, Bob Lafferty, glanced out an airplane window on a short hop out of Jakarta and noticed the long shadow of gargantuan reef angling off the southeastern tip of Java. After a battle of bad roads and worse boating, he and some friends found their way to what was soon to become G-Land, short for Grajagan, the world's first jungle surf camp. In 1974 Tony Hilde and Mark Scanlon hitched a ride out of Goa, India, and ended up shipwrecked and surfing in the Maldives. In 1975 it was Lagundri Bay, Nias, and five years later the Mentawai Islands, off the coast of Sumatra, a discovery that had by this point become so routine that the *Outside* magazine writer Rob Story called its uncovering "good old surf imperialism."

Certainly these things would have happened without *The Endless Summer,* but not nearly as quickly and not with the same sense of purpose. Because of the movie's influence, because folks heeded its call, surfing went from being a backyard pastime to a worldwide quest. While no quantitative data explains the mind-shift that accompanied this transition, it's a safe assumption that the surf quest, the most fundamental element found in the Conductor's story, did not exist in any serious form before 1964. It wasn't much, but it was a place to start.

16

My journey to Bruce Brown's house took a little more than five hours or a little less than eleven years depending on when you start the clock. If you start the clock around seven in the morning on the sunny, summer day when I drove north from Los Angeles to a spot twenty-five miles north of Santa Barbara, it annoyingly took more than five hours. It should have taken less than three, but we got lost. We got lost because the directions Bruce's son, Dana Brown, left on my voice mail were an address off Highway One and a cryptic addendum: "If you pass the *Blade Runner*-looking refinery you've gone too far." I was thirty-six years old and certain that I'd passed the *Blade Runner*-looking refinery a long time ago.

I was driving with a friend to meet Brown because, a few weeks prior, Dana had released his first film, *Step into Liquid,* the hypothetical third installment in what would become *The Endless Summer* trilogy. Both my friend and myself had seen the film and conspired to write as much as possible about both men because both men had become beacons in our respective personal mythologies. Writing stories about such beacons is what journalists do to give meaning to their lives. Which is to say, I was driving north from Los Angeles not just because a couple of guys had made a couple of movies, but because, in the middle of a freezing Baltimore winter, when I wanted nothing as much as I wanted California sunshine, I read Kem Nunn's *Tapping the Source.*

I read *Tapping the Source* in graduate school, studying creative writing under the unusual tutelage of Robert Stone. By that point, Stone was already a literary legend, both a National Book Award winner and one of the last living Merry Pranksters, but one not built for the rigors of academia. He was often given to wild flights. On the first day of class, Stone walked in, sat down, said little, read James Joyce's "Araby" aloud, in its entirety, closed the book, closed his eyes for about thirty seconds, opened his eyes, stood up, said good-bye and left. What went on in his mind during those thirty seconds was anyone's guess.

During that same period, I was making ends meet tending bar. I met a local surfer, Derek I think his name was, who told me there were waves breaking on Maryland's Eastern Shore. I hadn't yet been on a board. He had an extra wetsuit, offered to teach me, and did so the hard way. He gave me a shortboard and no instructions. I paddled headlong into nasty shorebreak, and the first wave I met snapped the pointed nose of the surfboard into the soft flesh of my cheek. I got out of the water as fast as I got in. A few days later Stone saw the cut, asked after it. I told him the story, and he told me to read *Tapping the Source*.

Nunn's book, part hard-boiled fiction, part tale of watery redemption, was set at a mythical place called the Ranch, somewhere north of Santa Barbara and south of Shangri-La. The Ranch, in Nunn's book, was a cattle ranch that abutted the finest waves in California, the break kept safe and secret by a group of heavily armed cowboys. At the time I first read the book, I had no idea if the Ranch even existed. In the years after, even when surfing in nearby San Francisco, no one had ever mentioned it. Then, years later, I was on the phone with Dana Brown, discussing the possibility of an interview, when he said, "Why don't you drive up the coast, you can interview me, meet my father, and we'll all go surf the Ranch."

I didn't need to be asked twice. A few days later my friend and

I were lost, doing fruitless laps on the Pacific Coast Highway, passing the *Blade Runner*–looking refinery again and again when we finally spotted a police cruiser parked in a turnout, just off the road. We pulled alongside the car and glanced through the open window at the cop, who was sleeping with his jaw open and a bulbous nose so veiny that it looked like a booze-broken road map to every sadsack tavern in California. We woke him up and asked him if he knew the address we needed.

"No" giving us his best hard-cop onceover—"wouldn't know where that is."

"Umm, we're looking for Bruce Brown's place."

Then he noticed the surfboards strapped to our roof. "Oh, that figures."

He gave us directions to an expansive ranchero nestled far back from the road, at the base of a deep canyon. Just past the backyard, a rocky outcropping stood like a sentinel atop a steep cliff. The Pacific was visible from the front porch. Brown had bought the land back before anyone realized that coastal property near Santa Barbara was going to become what coastal property near Santa Barbara became. He lived there with his wife and dog and endured frequent visitors. We walked in as both Dana and Bruce Brown and Robert "Wingnut" Weaver, the iconoclastic Santa Cruz longboarder made famous by *The Endless Summer II,* were recording commentary to accompany the release of that movie's DVD. Bruce told us to grab a beer from the fridge and make ourselves at home. It was about noon, perhaps as good a time as any to start drinking.

Bruce, tanned and talkative and nearing his middle sixties, sat on a couch, speaking in the same laconic rhythm found in all his films. For the better portion of an hour, we asked surf questions, and he told surf stories. We learned that the plane crash at the end of *The Endless Summer II* wasn't staged, and that the lion tamer who appeared in that film had recently been eaten by lions. We hit golf balls from the front lawn into the canyon beyond and, a little while later, packed into Wingnut's van and set out for never-never land.

The Ranch remains a California myth. It doesn't appear on most maps, and no signs point the way from the freeway. The land was first purchased by the Hollister family in the mid-nineteenth century and kept intact, as a functioning cattle ranch, until the late 1960s. Financial difficulties and bickering heirs finally forced the sale of fourteen thousand acres. These were then opened for development with iron-clad strictures put into place: the land was split into 140 plots, each a hundred acres long, and could not be further subdivided. Purchase prices started out high and soon became extraordinary, taking the notion of a gated community to its logical extreme. Today, outsiders can legally boat in from nearby harbors, but direct access to the beach is reserved for landowners and enforced by both a fierce localism and an armed guard at the gate. The point being that the Ranch's fabled waves are the ultimate secret spot and meant to stay that way.

Considering everything, the drive over should have felt like an event, but it was truly uneventful. Six-packs were bought at a general store. At the Ranch's gate, Wingnut stopped to chat with an old surf buddy who had unplugged himself from the grind and taken a job working this remote post. We drove on, climbed hills, logged miles on a winding road, ten minutes, twenty, the coastline visible only in snatches.

The swell was too small. Neither the Ranch's fabled Rights or Lefts were working, so we spent a bit of time standing on bluffs looking out over the water and, after much discussion, settled on Auggie's, a snapping A-frame of a wave that had little snap that day. Unpacking the car, Wingnut took one look at the old wax coat on my board and pronounced it disrespectful to the sport of surfing, which was a little bit like Jesus showing up to tell some backwoods parish priest he didn't know how to conduct a mass. I felt self-conscious about adding more, and because of this, for the rest of the afternoon, I could barely keep my footing, but that didn't matter since I had also followed Wingnut's masochistic lead and not bothered to put on a wetsuit, instead paddling out in board trunks and a rash guard in water that turned out to be several degrees above freezing.

So I was freezing and slipping and slipping and freezing, and that was how the day went. My friend got a couple of rides; Dana got a couple of rides; Wingnut caught pond ripples and rode them for fifty yards at a time. I got nothing beyond a long look at my own personal mythology turned inside out. I had embarked on a quest for surf with the very men who had invented the idea of questing for surf and not managed to catch a wave. Was there a lesson to be learned here?

Hard to say.

17

It was the first big winter swell. The water temperature had dropped ten degrees since Thanksgiving, but it didn't matter. The breaks were crowded up and down the coast. The first big winter swell served as a clarion call that all the old-school salt dogs answered. I surfed three consecutive days, and always the lineups were thick with boards shaped in other decades and the men who rode them.

The first day was a Friday. I started out at the slam pit of Topanga, where the canyon of that same name poured out of the Santa Monica Mountains and down into the Pacific. Topanga was elbow-to-elbow and ego-to-ego, and the irony of it was that most of the people there considered surfing a religious experience and that their religious experience was being ruined by all the others surfing for the same reason. Being at Topanga on the first day of the first big winter swell was like watching pilgrims fistfight at Mecca. It was too much to handle. I got one wave an hour for two hours and went home.

The following morning, I went north to Staircase, a wonderful A-frame wave up near the Ventura County line. The last time I had surfed this far north, the Santa Anas were blowing and the California fires were burning. Smoke stained the sky a deep purple. Almost no one was out. I traded waves with three other guys, who talked about how happy they were that the fires were burning.

"The freeways are closed," one said.

"People can't make it to the ocean," clarified another.

"It's not that I mind other surfers," continued the first. "I mind the attitudes. God makes waves aplenty; people just need to remember that."

At Staircase, on the Saturday of the first big winter swell, memories were once again failing. The next day was Sunday; a friend and I spent our day of rest driving south toward San Diego. We wanted to go to Swamis, one of the best-named waves in California. This naming of waves is a tricky business. Some are known for their proximity to familiar landmarks. North of Los Angeles is a spot called Heavens, because the beach bathrooms found there are among the cleanest in California. Geographic names are also common. The wave Nusa Dua is located in the place Nusa Dua. Others are known for personalities or predominant characteristics. The big wave Jaws for its ferocity; the legendary Pipeline because it looks like a giant pipe. *Cloudbreaks* are rare waves found in the middle of the ocean, where the crashing foam looks like clouds from a distance; while a *zero break* is a rarely seen big wave that breaks far from the shore. But the question remains: what is actually being named here?

Waves are weather. Going surfing is the rough equivalent of going to visit a thunderstorm. Just as no two thunderstorms are the same, no two waves are the same. So what's really being named is our recognition of a pattern. Temperature produces wind, which produces waves, which interact with a near infinite number of variables to produce something that we find consistently recognizable despite being absolutely temporary and completely variable. And because surfing takes place at such high speeds on such a wildly variable surface, the sport requires an incredible amount of muscle memory. Muscle memory is created when a movement is repeated so many times that it forms a pattern that then becomes a permanent feature of our brain's subconscious database. This means that much of surfing is the experience of a subconscious pattern interacting with an ineffable pattern—whatever the hell that means.

I once called Jim White to talk about what the hell that means, and he pointed out that it's not even the wave that's being named, but the last expression of that wave's life. "You're riding on a dying wave. Every wave will eventually hit a sandbar or a reef and start to break. You catch a wave at the apex of its life, at the moment it begins to fulfill its final destiny, and the ride ends when that wave has fulfilled that destiny. What's really going on when surfing is actually a kind of shared death dance. That's also the really ineffable part about the names of waves, because the experience of that shared death dance is also what's being named."

Swamis itself is named for the Self-Realization Fellowship's gold-domed temple that sits atop the bluff overlooking the break. The temple was built for Swami Paramahansa Yogananda in 1937, but the wave has become the bigger draw. On the day we went, there were two hundred guys in the water at Swamis. There was to be no enlightenment that day. We drove a mile farther south and paddled out at Cardiff Reef.

Normally, on a day when the waves were well overhead, I would think twice about paddling into a crowded lineup at Cardiff Reef. It was a question of ability. It's one thing to scream into those waves; it's another to scream into them at Cardiff, where six other guys join you for the ride. Errors have consequences, and Lyme was hell on balance. But I was on the trail of the Conductor. That was that. I paddled out.

Of all the things I was training, it was my stance that was the most troubling. I had what surfers politely reference as *stink butt*. In other words, when I surfed, I looked a lot like a guy trying to ride waves and shit bricks simultaneously. I had the wide-footed squat of a Sumo wrestler and no idea how to fix it. For three months I'd been thinking about it but had gotten no closer to an answer.

"You've got stink butt," my friend said after we had come back to the beach.

"Yeah."

"You need to turn your back foot in more, to point into the wave with your knee."

"Really?"

"Yeah, really."

"No, I mean, that's all, it's that simple."

"Yeah, it's that simple."

Apparently, I was wrong. There was a little enlightenment to be had after all. Little victories. We take them where we can.

18

Most historians date the arrival of Eastern religious thought on American shores to October 4, 1965, the day LBJ took the podium on Liberty Island, under the long shadow of the good lady herself, and made a few brief remarks to commemorate the signing of a new bill. Among other things said that day, the president noted: "This bill . . . is not a revolutionary bill. It does not affect the lives of millions. It will not reshape the structure of our daily lives, or really add importantly to either our wealth or our power." On this, and other things, the president was wrong. It was a sign of the times perhaps; the sixties were a decade when plenty of men paid their rent by seriously underestimating a couple of Asians with a couple of ideas of their own.

The bill was the Immigration and Naturalization Act of 1965, and it put an end to restrictive quota systems that existed to ensure that "we the people" meant, mostly, we the white people. Instead, the act based entrance into the United States upon skills, giving preference to those with the means to support themselves, or those with relatives already living in America. LBJ saw it as an idealistic gesture. In his mind, it was nothing more or less than the way a great nation should behave.

Almost immediately after the bill's signing, spiritual leaders from religious traditions far beyond the Judeo-Christian playground began arriving in America. In 1965, Swami A. C. Bhaktivedanta

Prabhupada took up chanting "Hare Krishna, Hare Rama" in Tompkins Square Park, months later expanding the operation into the International Society for Krishna Consciousness, which, in turn, grew steadily, bringing *shikha* haircuts and jangle-jangle tambourines to airports across the land and giving many a parent one more damn thing to worry about. In 1966, Allen Ginsberg published his aptly and irresistibly titled "Wichita Vortex Sutra," while Maharishi Mahesh Yogi taught Transcendental Meditation to anyone who asked—and later, thanks to the Beatles, plenty who didn't. By 1968, the words *Vedic literature* had entered the lexicon of polite cocktail hour conversation. In 1969, Swami Satchidananda chanted for the children of Woodstock, and Yogi Bhajan revealed the secrets of kundalini to the kind of adults who couldn't tell their chakras from their old socks. In 1970, it was Baba Muktananda and Siddha Yoga Dham and Swami Rama. That same year, Swami Rama paid a visit to the Menninger Foundation in Topeka, Kansas, and demonstrated his yogic prowess by stopping his heart for an assembly of gathered scientists, the EKG of which, as it appears in *Beyond Biofeedback,* by Elmer and Alyce Green, shows both the atrial flutter that preceded cessation and the sharp downward spike of stone-cold stoppage.

During this period, a number of Islamic variations also made an appearance, as did nearly every lineage of Buddhism save Zen, which had already been around for a while: introduced back in the fifties by Gary Snyder, well publicized and possibly bastardized by Jack Kerouac's band of coffeehouse poets, the result of which was dismissed by Alan Watts as faddish and rank, calling it "Beat Zen" and other such names. But the sixties brought Zen back and every other dharma lineage known to man. So many that Los Angeles has since become home to more Buddhist sects than any other city on the planet.

In total, the impact of the Immigration and Naturalization Act on America's spiritual identity was so completely transformative that religious historians refer to it as the "Watershed of 1965." The end result, as documented by the Harvard scholar Diana Eck in her book *A New Religious America,* was that within twenty-five years the United States had become "the most religiously diverse nation on earth." As a new survey by the Ontario Consultants on Religious Tolerance points out, if American pluralism continues at its present pace, by the year 2042, non-Christians will outnumber Christians in the United States.

Possibly because the need for ecstatic transformative experience is not a visible malady, the act's impact caught plenty besides LBJ by surprise. Barring a few errant souls, America came out of the fifties a spiritually strangled place. The magic had long vanished from that old-time religion, replaced by rational materialism's promises of atomic worlds and medicinal cures, conquests considered holy by an excitable breed of secular mystics, but not quite as spiritually fulfilling as many wanted.

As for the mechanics behind that want, well, hundreds of scholars have documented the reasons behind the loss of Western civilization's archaic heritage, finding fault in any number of sweeping directions, but whether you want to blame the power politics of the priest class or the rise of the machine age or the institutionalization of faith or any other deaths by a thousand cuts, by the fifties, American spirituality had become a dry Sunday pastime.

Things only got worse as the sixties rolled around. All across the country, the people had grown restless and curious and hungry for revolution, spiritual or otherwise. Vast swatches of the populous were starting to realize the depth of disconnect between their government's words and deeds, turning distrust of any and all establishments, organized religion principal among them, into more than just a disaffected stance. Psychedelics got tossed into this mix, and while many are quick to discount their effects, the drugs taught many that when it comes to reality, things are not always what they seem. A fact which soon brought Norman Mailer's "armies of the night" to the Pentagon, surrounding it with hopes of levitation and other insights.

As Theodore Roszak pointed out in his *The Making of a Counter Culture,* "the dissenting youth have indeed got religion," and then went on to further explain:

> Zen, Sufism, Hinduism, primitive shamanism, theosophy, the Left-Handed Tantra . . . The Berkeley "wandering priest" Charlie (Brown) Artman, who was running for city councilman in 1966 until he was arrested for confessing (quite unabashedly) to possession of narcotics, strikes the right note of eclectic religiosity: a stash of LSD in his Indian-sign necklace, a chatelaine of Hindu temple bells, and the campaign slogan "May the baby Jesus open your mind and shut your mouth." Satanists and Neo-Gnostics, dervishes and self-proclaimed swamis . . . their number grows and the counter culture makes generous place for them.

And perhaps no place was found more generous than the surf community, where marginalization had long been more of the rule than the exception anyway. "Ignoring a brief period of mainstream popularity during the Gidgit era, surfing has always been a renegade act," Paul Holmes, an editor at *Longboard* magazine, once told me. "In the late forties and fifties, if you were a committed surfer, you didn't work, you weren't a citizen, you hung out at the beach all day and spear-fished for dinner. You pried abalone off rocks and slept on the sand." By the time the papers got around to mentioning that hippie phenomenon, out at the beach they were already ass-deep in free love and bell-bottoms and funky religion.

Around the time Mailer's night armies descended on the

nation's capital, Tom Wolfe was in California, hanging out with a band of surfers known as the Pump House Gang: Liz, who was into necromancy, and Larry, who "spent two years with a monk, and he learned a lot of stuff," and all the rest of them. Out at the beach the kids were always using the word *mysterioso* to denote "the perfect alchemical combination of mystical and hip." "It refers to the mystery of the Oh Mighty Hulking Pacific Ocean and everything" was how Wolfe put it.

"Back then everybody was trying to raise their consciousness," said the legendary surfer and board shaper Dick Brewer. "A lot of them tried it with drugs—there were a lot of drugs—but other methods as well." Brewer himself studied Zazen in Hawaii, at a tiny temple near Hanapepe, later teaching surfers Gerry Lopez and Reno Abellira to meditate, a feat commemorated in David Darling's famous "Lotus" photo of the trio cross-legged and closed-eyed in a little park on Mount Tantalus.

It was also Brewer who had "cheap *Kensho*," a brief moment of white light and pure enlightenment, during a formal weeklong meditation marathon at a monastery on Oahu. Afterward, the famed 113-year-old Zen master Yosefari Roshi took Brewer aside and pronounced him the only enlightened Westerner. It was a pronouncement I had always wondered about, so a while back I called Brewer at his home in Hawaii to find out if the Roshi meant that he was the only enlightened Westerner or if he meant the only enlightened Westerner he had ever met. "No," said Brewer, "he meant the only one." Brewer is generally credited with pioneering the radical shortboard design that gave rise to all of modern surfing, a feat which occurred two weeks after he attained his enlightenment, however brief.

And it was into this mix that Bruce Brown released *The Endless Summer*. For a smaller subset of the subculture these ideas began to blend: the surf quest becoming the spiritual quest and vice versa. This led to an era when surfers would routinely take hits of acid and paddle out in the biggest waves they could find, an experience described by Bill Hamilton in Drew Kampion's *The Way of the Surfer*: "I sat on my surfboard feeling the ocean going through my spine and bathing my head with its warmth." Hamilton went on to note "that if there was any benefit of that, the psychedelic era, it was that it opened our Western minds to Eastern forms of thought and belief and philosophy and a really interesting kind of thinking." And while I couldn't be sure, it seemed like just the kind of society where newly minted mythical tales—like the story of the Conductor—could take hold and begin to spread.

Both the release of *The Endless Summer* and the passage of the Immigration and Naturalization Act took place in the middle sixties. It seemed a pretty safe bet that the Conductor's legend emerged at some point afterward, but if I wanted to be certain, it would help to know what the weather was doing during this period. What was the general public feeling about meteorology? What was the surf community thinking about it? Was anyone anywhere thinking about weather control? I didn't want to know the external climate as much as I wanted to know the influence that external climate had on our internal climate. It wasn't so much that I was looking for a surfer who could control the weather; it was that I was looking for a point in time when people might be willing to entertain a fantasy about a surfer who could control the weather.

19

For nearly as long as there have been gods there have been climate-controlling gods. Even the list of deities who specialize in thunderwork runs long: the Hindu Indra; the German Donar; the Byelorussian Pjarun; the Finnish Ukko, whose name means both "thunder" and "old man" and is often used as a term of respect; stormy, Roman Jupiter, whose vengeance was considered a sign of condemnation, and thus those felled by lightning during his reign were denied proper burial; the legendary Thor, whose name has twisted over time into "thunder"; African and Pacific Island deities with names that feel strange in our mouths—Vayu, Summanus, Umpundulo, Adad, Wakinyan, Tanka—and on and on.

And as long as the lists of gods runs, the list of humans who have used magic to try to control the weather is much longer. The earliest recorded attempts belong to the Aztecs, who performed human sacrifices in AD 500 in their bid to wrench wet rain from dry skies. In *The Golden Bough,* Sir James George Frazer devotes an entire chapter to such occurrences, declaring, "Of the things which the public magician sets himself to do for the good of the tribe, one of the chief is to control the weather." And thus from every corner of the earth come such stories. Among my favorites are the Dieri people of central Australia, who would save foreskins culled from tribal youths during ritual circumcisions so they could later bury them in the desert to summon the rain; the northern

Europeans, who captured the wind in bags tied up with string; and the early Christians, who augmented an old and traditional idea, that the gods can hear us, and thus they rang holy bells furiously to ward off bad weather—a practice which, owing to the design of church spires and the proclivity of lightning for such spires, led to an incredibly high mortality rate among bell ringers.

Running concurrent with these mythic theories was an attempt at a serious scientific tradition. Around 650 BC, the Babylonians began short-term climate forecasting, and three hundred years later, Chinese astronomers had advanced the process far enough that they could divide the year into twenty-four weather-shaped parts. In 340 BC, Aristotle penned *Meteorologica*, a four-volume treatise which soon became the core text on the subject. Aristotle believed that four elements—earth, fire, air and water—intertwined to create various weather-related phenomena of the world. This produced some rather odd results. Everything from earthquakes to streaking comets were considered meteorological events, classified by the philosopher as dry exhalations of the planet. Despite having as much in common with reality as the Easter Bunny, *Meteorologica*'s hegemonic reign ran for twelve hundred years until the very basic errors in his work led scientists to conclude that some better tools for observation were required.

Satisfying this need were a series of inventions—Nicholas of Cusa's humidity-measuring hygrometer from the mid-fifteenth century, Galileo Galilei's 1592 invention of the thermometer and Evangelista Torricelli's mid-sixteenth-century barometer—all of which had permanent and far-reaching effects. For a long while these tools of measurement served a dual function, allowing people to pursue science under the veil of pursuing religion. It wasn't that the hygrometer could measure humidity; it was that God created humidity and the hygrometer could help us to better understand God's creation. Scholars call this transformative pursuit of knowledge the

Age of Enlightenment, but it was also a winnowing of religion. It wasn't just that *the gods* had become *the God* (a process which began with the emergence of monotheism, during Babylonian times, and became strategic and codified as first Judaism and later Christianity and then Islam began to spread), but that the deist idea of God as prime mover—He who set things in motion but could no longer or chose to no longer influence the outcome—gained favor. Either way, our knowledge of God's weather didn't coalesce until the eighteenth and nineteenth centuries, when the combination of these more precise instruments and new theories of evaporation and condensation led to mildly accurate forecasting.

The real breakthrough came in 1845, when Samuel Morse made the telegraph commercially viable and, within fifteen years, allowed for another possibility: global weather forecasting. In 1870, President Ulysses S. Grant signed a joint resolution of Congress authorizing the secretary of war to establish the Army Signal Service Corps and on November 1 of that year to begin taking systematized and synchronous meteorological reports. The information was individually gathered and then transmitted to a central office in Washington, D.C., where it was condensed into our first national weather report. And it was this, the telegraph—and the networks of weather observatories linked by telegraph—that moved weather from the realm of unknowable mystery to knowable mystery.

A few years past the emergence of these telegraph networks, the idea of weather control as a strictly human pursuit came into play. Gone were the circumcisions and bell ringing and fancy dancing. One of the world's oldest mystical traditions—the shamanic control of the weather—had started becoming our newest hard science. Though how hard was a matter of perspective.

In 1896, a locally famous Austrian wine grower, Albert Stiger, decided to test the world's first hail cannon. Hail was a serious problem for European wine growers, and the hail cannon was the best that science could offer by way of a solution. It was a three-hundred-foot-tall cone, the narrow end pointed at the ground and the wide mouth pointed at the sky. The cannon was muzzle loaded and used to shoot mortars into the clouds. The hope was that this would prevent hail by forcing smoke into the clouds, and thereby creating billions of tiny nuclei upon which moisture would condense. The now heavier moisture would then fall to the earth as harmless rain rather than harmful hail. This was cutting-edge science at the time, and, as often is the case in weather control, coincidence conspired against reality.

During that first year, 1896, Stiger fired six cannons skyward and triumphantly; no hail fell. Nearby villagers, buoyed by his success, erected thirty more cannons in the surrounding countryside. They proceeded to spend much of 1897 firing smoke rings at clouds. No hail fell that year either. Other Europeans, believing in the veracity of these results, began purchasing cannons to protect their own crops. During 1899, what has come to be called "cannon fever" swept the continent. All of Austria and Germany got caught up; Italy bragged it had two thousand cannons and the willingness to use them.

To understand the rise of cannon fever is to understand that two shamanic ideas—that the gods could hear us and that loud noises frightened the gods—had merged with a scientific idea—that firing smoke into clouds could heat hail into water, which would then fall as rain. It wasn't that thousands of Europeans were suddenly hip to new science; it was that this new science was a blend of traditionally accepted religious ideas with a more modern twist. In the end it didn't matter. Europeans could fire all the canons they wanted; the weather could care less. Hail fell anyway. The fever quieted as quickly as it had risen.

It was also during this time that the inventor Nikola Tesla, most famous for his discovery of AC current (the basis for all of our electrical systems), began publishing his ideas about weather manipulation (heating the ionosphere—the portion of the upper atmosphere extending thirty-five to five hundred miles above the earth's surface—with radio waves to produce catastrophic effects), scalar weapons (a technique for heating the ionosphere to produce catastrophic effects that many believe led to the idea behind Ronald Reagan's now famous and failed Star Wars initiative) and wireless radio waves (more or less what they sound like, wireless radio waves). The arguments about Tesla's work have raged for the better portion of a hundred years and will most likely rage for a hundred more. Even a small step into his world quickly plunges one down the raw rabbit hole of conspiracy theory, where the rules of physics seem to have been replaced by dandy illogic—but more on that later.

People date the modern history of weather modification to November 13, 1946, the day when Vincent Schaefer, Bernard Vonnegut (brother to the writer Kurt) and Irving Langmuir, all scientists working out of General Electric's research laboratory in Schenectady, New York, created—to quote Barrington S. Havens, GE's official historian—the "first man-made snowstorm." They did so by dumping three pounds of pulverized dry ice from an airplane into a heavy bank of clouds. The dry ice caused the water vapor within the cloud to form ice crystals, which then grew heavier and heavier until, about five minutes later, it began to snow. Thus the modern technique for cloud seeding had been invented.

Those five minutes, the waiting period between cloud seeding and snow falling, bring to mind these words of e.e. cummings: "We have wintered the death of the old, cold year." Five minutes— the gap between cloud seeding and snow falling. Three hundred seconds—a little more than most can hold their breath. That was how long it took. The fall of an empire of context, the time it took humans to catch gods.

STEVEN KOTLER

Of course, GE's initial experiment led to others. On the last day of their first two-month trial, another cloud bank was seeded. Almost immediately, record snows began to fall, burying most of upstate New York. These days we know enough about atmospheric science to call this a coincidence, but at the time people weren't so sure. By 1947, dry ice was replaced with silver iodine, producing even better results. A few months later, GE teamed with the U.S. Military for a project code-named Cirrus. For the better portion of five years, under that apt moniker, 264 experiments were conducted in fifteen sites from Puerto Rico to Hawaii. All forms of weather modification were tried, but the most famous of those attempts took place on October 13, 1947, when Project Cirrus dropped eighty kilograms of dry ice into a hurricane off America's East Coast. The hope was that cloud seeding would alter its direction, which it did, but unfortunately in the wrong direction. The hurricane turned inland, overrunning much of Georgia.

We now know enough about tropical storm movement to understand that the hurricane had already altered its path, long before the seeding, but that kind of information required both serious cloud physics and the aid of supercomputers—and neither was available in 1947. The Associated Press caught wind of this story, and others soon followed. On November 10, *Time* magazine reported: "In Savannah last week, Southern blood bubbled toward the boiling point. A Miami weatherman had hinted that last month's disastrous hurricane might not have been an act of God, but just a low Yankee trick."

And there, in a sentence, was the hinge. For nearly three thousand years, weather had been the province of the gods. For a little more than three hundred years, it had become a more human territory, but in that one sentence, in those few words—*a Yankee trick*—we went off to the races. There are a great number of ways to look at the intersection of science and religion, but inevitably, in every such merger, there comes a point when paths cross and further diverge. Usually, one of these divergent streams heads underground, out of sight, where it is carried on a current of hearsay and paranoia, only to emerge later as conspiracy theory. The other heads aboveground, into the plain sight of discussion and argument and eventually, when all else fails, politics.

In weather modification, this change took less than four years. In 1950, fearing serious litigation, GE stopped all its experiments, but others continued. A few years later, a rainmaker was hired to seed clouds in the Catskill Mountains in response to a water shortage in New York City. Soon afterward, a Catskill country club sued the city for scaring off vacationers. In one of the odder rulings ever produced, the State's Supreme Court decided that the thirsty city of New York had priority over a private club. By 1955, three new bills, all attempting to regulate weather modification, were working their way through Congress. Bernard Vonnegut, in a written statement read aloud at the hearings, said, "The potentialities, both for good and bad, which attend silver-iodine seeding are so large that the development and use of this technique must be placed in the hands of the Federal Government."

But it was an internal memo, written by Langmuir, that set the stage for what happened next. "The possibility of wide-scale control of weather conditions, of course, offers important military applications." And by the late fifties, as the cogs of the Cold War began slipping into gear, U.S. intelligence gatherers began hearing buzz of a Russian weather control program, rumored to be based on Tesla's designs. In 1957, the Presidential Advisory Committee on Weather Control pointed out that "weather modification could become a more important weapon than the atom bomb." And before that decade's end, working out of the navy's China Lake weapons research center, the U.S. government had a full-scale weather modification program up and running.

By the midsixties, the CIA took notice, and in 1966 Project Popeye commenced. The idea was to cloud-seed Vietnam in hopes of turning the Ho Chi Minh Trail to impassable mud and thus destroying enemy supply lines. In July of 1972, Seymour Hersh broke word of Popeye on the front page of the *New York Times*, but the White House kept mum on the subject. Its silence fueled rumors of conspiracy. And if this were simply a tale of attempts at weather modification, our story would just about come to a close. By 1977, the House ratified the Convention of the Publication of Military or Any Other Hostile Use of Environmental Modification Techniques (ENMOD), an international treaty banning such activities that still stands today.

Following its ratification—and for good reason—most of these activities dried up. The truth of that matter was that weather proved to be too big for science. The final conclusion of Project Cirrus and much of what followed was that if preexisting conditions were perfect, the chance of rain could be increased by 5 to 10 percent. Hurricanes could not be shifted. Deserts could not be watered. Even lowly fog could not be dissipated. We had run into the wall of ignorance. Scientists gave up. They took a path not open to theologians: they said, "We don't know."

This is not just a story of fact but also a trail of belief. And it is much easier to control what happens than what is thought. The problem with saying "We don't know" is simply that. Humankind is fundamentally uneasy with unawareness. Why does the intersection of science and religion always lead to politics? Is it not a knee-jerk reaction to the limits of human knowledge, a way of buck passing that quickly tries to fill the vacuum of serious scientific ignorance? And in the seventies, when politicians refused to fulfill this duty, conspiracy theorists—who often share the fervor of the religiously devout—rushed to fill that gap. It was here where we found Tesla's ideas about weather modification, scalar weapons and wireless radio technology reemerging.

Between 1963 and 1982, the United States built the Omega Navigational Network, a multinational array of radio transmitters used to monitor the weather (basically an upgraded, high-tech version of Grant's Army Service Signal Corp), though you wouldn't know this from perusing the available data. An Internet search for the Omega system produces results like Joe Vitale's essay, "Tesla's Electromagnetic Pyramid," in which the author claims that Omega's navigation functions were actually a cover-up, hiding "the network's real purpose of subtly manipulating the resonant frequency of the earth itself." Meaning that the folks in charge of Omega—at least according to the conspiracy theorists—would also control the weather.

But Omega was only the beginning. In the early nineties, to research the ionosphere, the U.S. government began building the High-Frequency Active Auroral Research Program (HAARP) in Gakona, Alaska. That HAARP has military applications is not in question. It's a Pentagon-sponsored project, intended to expand knowledge about the nature of long-range radio communications and surveillance—mainly with the hope of bettering submarine communications and detecting foreign missile launches—but in less than ten years, HAARP replaced Omega as the nexus of weather control conspiracy theory.

There is a plethora of conspiracy literature—from scholarly books to dedicated Web sites—that reveals HAARP's true purpose: a combination weather control device (apparently, the U.S. government caused Mount St. Helens to explode, though why the government would test its weather control device on its own soil seems a more difficult question to answer) and Star Wars technology (apparently, a souped-up version of HAARP can shoot down incoming missiles).

In 1996, the U.S. Air Force released a detailed report titled *Weather as a Force Multiplier: Owning the Weather in 2025,* explaining that by augmenting existing weather modification techniques with sure-to-come technological advances like nanotech-based artificial weather, the United States could use rain and sleet and snow to "shape the battlespace in ways never before possible."

The report's cover gives the start date for these weather weapons as 2025, which may be a little premature since weather control is still considered the bastard child of meteorology. Cloud seeding and other such pursuits are mostly unwelcome at science conferences, and articles about such topics are not favored with publication in the major peer-review journals. So unless you believe that most every scientist around is lying in a sanctioned and concerted effort to distort the truth, then, for a few more years at least, when a storm washes away the coast of Georgia, the question is not "why did it happen?" but "why do we believe what we believe about why it happened?"

It was in 1972 or 1973, a few months after the publication of Hersh's article, when the idea of weather control began to trickle out of laboratories and into the popular imagination. During the next ten years, bracketing the 1977 signing of ENMOD, weather control left pure science and birthed pure fantasy. By 1981, the notion had captured mainstream attention to such extent that the daytime soap opera *General Hospital* created the Ice Princess Saga, a lengthy plot line where our heroes—Luke and Laura—must battle the evil Cassadine brothers, who are scheming for world domination via a giant weather control machine.

I never expected to use daytime television to date the Conductor's myth, but at the time its weather control episodes were airing

General Hospital was the most popular soap opera in the history of soap operas. Thirty million viewers tuned in for Luke and Laura's wedding; a good portion of those also saw the Ice Princess Saga. Bruce Brown's 1964 release of *The Endless Summer* marked the earliest point a story about a surf quest could have emerged, and the 1965 passage of the Immigration and Naturalization Act opened the floodgates on Eastern mysticism. Both surfing and Eastern religion have only grown in popularity since their debut, becoming part of the common language by the late seventies—exactly the same time weather control was moving into the mainstream. This meant that three of the core ideas comprising the Conductor's myth were all in heavy circulation in the American psyche at the same time. This also meant that while I might still not know where the Conductor's tale first emerged, I was beginning to get a pretty good idea of when.

PART THREE

If this is all there is, then I definitely paid too much for this carpet.

—Woody Allen

20

In early April 2004, I found myself and my luggage in various states of undress in a back room in the Auckland International Airport. I had come to New Zealand because an Aussie surfer whose name I still can't remember told me about two surfers and a guy who conducts the waves and thought those two surfers just might be Kiwis. In subsequent conversations with a variety of historians there seemed to be something of a consensus opinion that the tale had a distinctly Polynesian flavor. Of the three and a half million people who live in New Zealand, 15 percent are Maori, while another six are a hodgepodge of Pacific Island heritages, giving this place the world's largest collection of likely suspects.

This wasn't much to go on, but then Bob Walter, the director of the Joseph Campbell Foundation and the editor of Campbell's *Historical Atlas of World Mythology,* opined that since weather modification was at the core of the Conductor's story, it was most likely a story that evolved from an early planting culture. It was agriculturalists, far more than hunter-gatherers, who needed to control the wind and rain. Most likely, Walter figured, it was a planting culture with a nautical flair and a strong history of fishing. There were a few that fit the bill, the Maori chief among them. These were the avenues I came to New Zealand to pursue, though what I expected to find remains a better question.

In hindsight, I suspect that my trip was less motivated by a need to find the origins of the Conductor's story than it was by a need to find what those surfers in the Conductor's story had found—a world where real magic was something more than mythological—but hindsight remains twenty-twenty and at the time I went to New Zealand I wasn't seeing anything very clearly. It would be convenient to explain my profound emotional fragility as one more symptom of illness—and there were plenty of times when I availed myself of this easy way out—but that would just be sleight of hand. In literature and cinema, as in life, I did not buy the one tragedy hypothesis. When I was in my early twenties, I dated a woman whose father had vanished when she was twelve. The last thing he did before leaving was douse their house with gasoline and light a match. He did this in the middle of the night, while his wife, young daughter and younger son were all still asleep in their beds. The young daughter would later grow into the young woman who I had been involved with and while there was plenty wrong with her life, she never once blamed her father. Which is to say, in the grand panoply of shit that could go wrong, a few years in the arms of ailment seemed a slight setback by comparison and definitely not something to ruin one's life over.

My problem wasn't the past; it was the future. Trying to track down the Conductor and trying to become a better surfer had become my way forward, but the myth's trail had grown cold and the weather as well. The winter rains had come early to California and would not quit. Storm drains had backed up and overflowed and turned the rivers to muck, and a light brown scum had been floating on the ocean for months. I already had Lyme disease and wasn't much interested in hepatitis, so had discovered the corollary to the whole surfing-saved-my life thesis: not surfing was kicking my ass.

Instead I got on a plane and flew to New Zealand, where there was plenty of great surf and no major pollution problems. I told myself that not being on a board for months shouldn't be too much of a concern, just like I told myself that flying halfway around the world on the trail of a myth was a perfectly reasonable endeavor. While I was pretty certain that I was lying to myself about the surfing, flying halfway around the world on the trail of a myth might have been a perfectly reasonable endeavor; there was just no way to tell. My compass was broken; my navigational skills were negligible. Plus, I couldn't step foot in New Zealand until I managed to clear customs—which wasn't as easy as it sounds.

When I was in fifth grade, among other things, I wanted to be a rock star. It was a transformation that somehow did not include playing a musical instrument but did include growing my hair long. Unfortunately, my hair is exceptionally and impossibly curly. It grows long as an Afro or in dreadlocks. I tried the Afro in high school and, in the years right after college, tried the dreads. The photo on my passport was taken during those later years, and, owing to the accumulation of stamps on its pages and a particular traveler's vanity that revolved around those stamps, I didn't want to trade it in for another. It didn't matter that my hair had been worn otherwise for nearly a decade; customs officials saw dreadlocks and thought drug dealer. So now I was sitting on a cold metal chair watching yet another customs official paw through my bags with what I have come to recognize as a certain feral glee.

He had already unpacked most of my bag and was now flipping through the books I had brought, finding nothing of note for a while and something extraordinarily fascinating around page 253 of Allan Weisbecker's *In Search of Captain Zero*. Possibly it was the line "I hadn't seen pussy in a while, never mind from the sort of gynecological angle I was afforded here," but I can't say for sure. When he shut the book, I decided it was a good time to ask if customs officials in New Zealand were always in the habit of picking on people with funny hair in their passport photos, or if it was more of an occasional happening.

"Just a random check," he said.

I was nearly barred entrance to the British Virgin Island because of that passport. In Rome, it earned me a strip search by a man of undeterminable age, squat and bald, with blubbery lips and palsy severe enough that he needed four tries to put on a rubber glove and two tries to gain entry. A few years after that, in an airport in Ecuador, I was waiting for my plane when twelve armed guards surrounded me and demanded to take me someplace quiet where they could search my luggage in peace. At the time, I happened to be traveling with my mother, who did not speak a lick of Spanish. Those guards spoke not a word of English. Watching my mother shout, "Where the hell are you taking my son?" while three inches from the business end of a Kalashnikov—absolutely, I was well acquainted with this kind of random check.

"Can I ask you something?" I said.

"Uh-huh."

"I flew in on a Boeing 747."

"Yeah?"

"It holds roughly five hundred people."

"So?"

"So we've all just gotten off the plane, and there's no one else in this room but the two of us."

He finished swabbing my drawers and moved on to tapping on my surfboard, and when that wasn't fun anymore he looked up at me and said, "Just a random check." He was a big guy with a mean stare, but I had nothing even vaguely circumspect in my bags and five hours until my connecting flight. There were no cool posters on the walls. I had to do something to pass the time.

"So let me ask you something else. I have dreadlocks in my

passport photo. We all know dreadlocks are universal code for drug dealer. I have stamps in there from Indonesia, Malaysia and Morocco. We all know those are three countries that foster and harbor terrorists. But since I know these things and I know that I have that passport, that would mean I would have to be an absolute idiot to try to smuggle anything into New Zealand."

"We're an equal-opportunity nation."

21

After customs came a puddle jumper to the city of Rotorua. I remember nothing of the flight and little of the airport beyond the young couple I saw outside the terminal. They were a few feet beyond the door, entwined in the kind of auspicious lovers' embrace one finds photographically represented in the dorm rooms of a certain type of college girl. I looked at them in the way that people look at other people at the start of long journeys. I had come halfway around the world on the trail of a ghost story. It felt farther away than the distance I had traveled. It felt like someone else's life.

The air was hot, heavy with the stink of sulfur. Rotorua marks the southern terminus of the Pacific Ring of Fire. Today there are three active volcanoes nearby and many theories. Shamans blamed the 1886 eruption of Mount Tarawera on the neglect of the old ways, specifically the local adoption of a cash economy. More recently, on Christmas Eve 1953, Ruapehu blew its top, causing a cascade of mud and lava that damaged a railway bridge that caused a train wreck that killed 151 people. When I asked a cab driver who was to blame for that flare-up, he said, "Way it goes around here." Along similar lines, in 1934, George Bernard Shaw visited Hell's Gate, one of many geothermal preserves in the area, and later regretted it, saying, "I wish I had never seen this place. It reminds me too vividly of the fate theologians have promised me."

I wanted to see Hell's Gate for myself but settled on the more centrally located Te Whakarewarewa, New Zealand's largest geo-thermal preserve. Te Whakarewarewa is actually an abridgement of Te Whakarewarewa o te Ope Taua a Wahiao, which my guidebook tells me means "the gathering together of the war party of Wahiao." The war party is long gone, but in its place sits the Maori Cultural Arts and Crafts Institute, where one can still learn the finer aspects of enemy disembowelment utilizing a Wahaika. There's also a replica Maori village, which includes native homes and meeting halls and an ice cream parlor and tourists in golf shirts and more children than should be allowed to congregate in one place. Guides in grass skirts only occasionally mention the traditional goods on sale in the gift shop. Beyond the village are pools of boiling water and bubbling mud and three active geysers. The air is thick with steam, the effect primal and anachronistic, part Mesozoic, part medieval, a lovely and dangerous land where one might comfortably confront either an Arthurian legend or a stegosaurus.

In the museum are display cases stocked with tribal wares: grass skirts, war clubs carved from whale bone, wooden hatchets elaborately ornamented, long spears, eel traps, jade worked into ornamental jewelry. The last great nomad ruler Temerlane—a Mogul who conquered more than anyone save Alexander the Great—believed that mornings were for war and afternoons for art. To these ends, in a synthesis of sorts, he built elaborate temples out of human bone. After wandering through the museum, I decided that the Maori were cut from the same cloth. Art and war. The two ways that humankind tried to elevate themselves above the mundane. I had a girlfriend once who thought she suffered from *minutiae*. It was a crippling, timeless ailment. Art and war. Two of the world's most certain cures for minutiae.

In another corner a dugout canoe that looks strapping and capable. The earliest Polynesian wave riders learned to surf to shore in boats such as these. In the seventeenth century Dutch explorers visiting New Zealand found the Maori riding waves in dugout canoes; by the eighteenth century it was English Calvinist missionaries and wooden planks. The missionaries quickly tried to put an end to the practice, just as they had in Hawaii, but one way or another people had been surfing here for a long time. It seemed a perfect place for a story like the Conductor's to take hold and ferment.

I wanted to ask someone about this, but there was no one around who looked like they had an answer. Instead, I decided that it was time to take a nap. I walked into the Institute's main office to get directions back to my hotel. A Maori woman well over six feet and several hundred pounds rose from her position behind a desk and stood tall and glowering and said, "Where you need to go, boy?"

I gave her the name of my hotel.

"You come with me."

She was much bigger than me, so there seemed no reason to argue. We walked out of the office and across the parking lot and piled into her car. She drove with two hands on the wheel, the windows down, the radio off. She wanted to know why I had come to her country. I knew she wanted to know this because she said, "Why you come, boy?" I told her the Conductor's story and mentioned that it might have a Maori connection. She never once looked away from the road.

22

Maori stories began as immigrant's tales retooled to fit New Zealand. They date back—well, the dates are unclear, but a long time ago, though not too long—to a time after the world's creation, after Tane Mahuta sculpted a woman out of red earth and breathed life into her nostrils and mated with her and had a daughter who later became his wife and bore him other daughters. After many other things like these had happened—most likely between AD 700 and 1000—Polynesians began spreading out across the Pacific in a series of migratory waves.

They navigated by bird flight, by starlight, traveling in canoes big enough to carry their old stories with them. Among those were the tales of the demigod Maui, a puckish raconteur of a child who lived in Hawaiki and one day went out fishing with his brothers. The fishhook he used was magical, carved from the jaw of his grandmother. Bone-carved versions are still worn ornamentally, a Maori symbol of authority and leadership, of deep knowledge of fishing and other important matters. It was on that day and with this fishhook that Maui caught Te Ika a Maui—the fish of Maui—known today as the North Island of New Zealand.

The following morning, I traveled the breath of Maui's catch, driving the road from Rotorua to Raglan, passing through a landscape hilly and verdant; this was the green carpet at the heart of New Zealand's agricultural industry. Sheep, by the hundreds, by the thousand, nibbled the grass short. Above it all was endless sky. When they first discovered New Zealand, the Polynesians called the land Aotearoa. Much of the time Aotearoa means "Long White Cloud," and some of the time "Land of the Long Day" or "Land of the Long Dawn" or "Land of the Long Twilight" and in certain cases "Long Bright World." I have yet to determine those cases, though all were in evidence on that drive.

I was traveling with a couple of California surfers both named John, neither of whom I knew well. One was a guy I knew from work, one was the friend of the guy I knew from work, both were good surfers, successful businessmen and ex–drug addicts—a combination, I assumed, that made them perfect traveling companions. Twenty years ago, one of the Johns had been down this road before. He pointed toward a set of distant mountains. To the right or the left of them—he couldn't be sure which—was the town of Raglan. He couldn't be sure which because in the time between his visits too much had changed, and for that surfing can claim plenty responsibility.

It was in Raglan, on Christmas day 1963, that Bruce Brown shot footage of Robert August riding a long left in what would soon become one of the cornerstone sequences in *The Endless Summer*. The shot shows August in classic longboarder style: standing tall and relaxed on the far front of his surfboard—nose-riding, as it is known—with his toes dangling off the edge and his board positioned perfectly in the curl. "The ride's so long it's ridiculous," says Brown in his voice-over narration. To prove that point, the shot goes on and keeps going on until it doesn't seem possible that this is the same shot of the same surfer on the same wave.

It was a shot that put Raglan in the middle of surfing lore. In the years since, it has become New Zealand's most famous break, still considered one of the world's best. The wave takes it name from the nearby town of Raglan, but that one word actually represents a collection of five separate surf spots: a beachbreak, a reefbreak and three different points. When the angle of the swell is matched by enough size, all of these link into a wave in excess of two miles. And when the wave is working, surfers come in droves.

In the years since Brown's visit, Raglan has grown from a few scant shacks into a picture-perfect beach community. "I remember years when it was just me and my mates in the water" is a rejoinder frequently heard from older surfers. While there are still only two main streets, as of late Aucklanders have taken to buying second homes here, as have Americans and other foreign nationals. The winter population hovers around three thousand; summer visitors quadruple that number on a busy weekend. So crowded has the break become that the surf company Volcom, which has a distributorship in town, recently printed bumper stickers that read: VOLCOM TO RAGLAN: NOW LEAVE.

The town itself takes it name from the ill-fated, one-armed British military leader Lord Raglan, whose troops were decimated during the Charge of the Light Brigade. Coincidentally, it was Raglan's great-grandson and namesake who wrote the 1936 mythic compendium *The Hero,* classifying patterns of typical mythical hero behavior into twenty-two archetypal incidents. Raglan's catalog is traditionally presented as a list, with each item counting for one point. The more points a particular hero scores on this scale, the closer he is to the mythic hero-king of prehistoric religious ritual.

1. The hero's mother is a royal virgin.
2. His father is a king and
3. often a near relative of the mother, but
4. the circumstances of his conception are unusual, and
5. he is also reputed to be the son of a god.
6. At birth an attempt is made, usually by his father or maternal grandfather, to kill him, but

7. he is spirited away, and
8. reared by foster parents in a far country.
9. We are told nothing of his childhood, but
10. on reaching manhood he returns or goes to his future kingdom.
11. After a victory over the king and/or giant, dragon, or wild beast,
12. he marries a princess, often the daughter of his predecessor, and
13. becomes king.
14. For a time he reigns uneventfully and
15. prescribes laws but
16. later loses favor with the gods and/or his people and
17. is driven from the throne and the city, after which
18. he meets with a mysterious death
19. often at the top of a hill.
20. His children, if any, do not succeed him.
21. His body is not buried, but nevertheless
22. he has one or more holy sepulchres.

On Raglan's Scale, Oedipus scores the highest of any mythic heroes, with Theseus, Moses and King Arthur as close runners-up. Robin Hood falls in the midrange for fictional characters, while Alexander the Great tops the list for historical figures. On Raglan's Scale, the Conductor scores not at all—though this may have more to do with my lacking a clear picture of the roots of the Conductor's story or the evolving nature of our mythological needs or some combination thereof. Anyway, there's little chance that Lord Raglan knew much about surfing. And while the Conductor's story was the technical reason for my trip, I was plenty keen to test myself on one of surfing's more fabled waves.

I was keen to test Raglan a few weeks shy of my thirty-seventh birthday, an age when my desire to be truly excellent at the sport of surfing was a desire that could easily be found on a scale a bit like Raglan's: twenty-two archetypal incidents that don't often happen to thirty-seven-year-old men. But the mythic is attractive because it straddles fact and fiction. And Raglan is a little of both. It's a steep, walling wave, mostly beyond my ability, whose tiny take-off spot perches atop a shallow rock shelf where an error means getting smashed onto that reef or swept onto the boulders that rim the shore. There are usually a few pros in the water and a local population who knows every inch of that wave, which means the only way to be assured a ride is to sit deep and drop fast, and while those skills are within my realm of possibility, they are not there frequently. When we finally got to Raglan and found the wind howling and the ocean sloppy, I was more than happy to go get some lunch.

We went to the Tongue and Groove Café, which sat a few miles back down the road, near the middle of town. The patrons were a mixed bag, and the warm mango chicken panini was excellent, even the fifth or sixth or seventh time ordered. The floor was worn and wooden and stained a lustrous black, and the walls were covered in surf paraphernalia and tribal masks and the kinds of paintings often found mixed in among surf paraphernalia and tribal masks. There were old couches and new couches and tables that looked like they had once been lost at sea and rows of theater seats repurposed for casual dining. The Johns liked it too, but I think that ultimately my fondness was really simple nostalgia. I had lost ten years to rooms just like this one.

At the front counter, I stood beside a regal woman, tall and lean, with her brown hair pinned up beneath a white sunbonnet. She wondered aloud if it was too early in the day to drink cham-pagne. I thought it was never too early to drink champagne and told her so. She told me that her grandmother had left England and come to Raglan some sixty years ago to spend a few thousand dollars on a few plots of land in an attempt to find a better life. No one in the family had ever come to visit and few knew the events of that better life, but the grandmother had recently died and willed this woman those same plots of land. Less than an hour ago, a real estate agent had informed her that her land was now worth well over a million dollars.

"We make our own luck," she said, "unless someone else makes it for us." She ordered champagne and drank it happily. I waited for a cup of coffee and read a New Zealand surf guide, which described Raglan as an advanced wave for two reasons: "surfers still get mangled jumping off the rocks" and "the crowds." One way or another, I was going to need plenty of luck.

23

Charlie Young was in his late forties, built like a fireplug, with messy brown hair and a serious fondness for Jack Daniels. He grew up in California, a surfer, teaching the sport at the Mission Bay aquatic center in San Diego before becoming a contract negotiator for the Long Beach Longshoreman's Union. In 1998, he and his wife, Erin, came to New Zealand on vacation and decided to never go home again. Back in the States, she owned a restaurant. They sold it and had enough other money saved to buy a patch of land atop a hill overlooking the break at Raglan.

The Youngs started out small and expanded. Now they own over a hundred acres of land and operate the Raglan Surf School and a hotel of sorts. On the acres they had built a series of rental cottages with names like Dream Catcher and Spin Palace and, for those on a budget, the Karioi Lodge: a sprawling backpacker's hostel taken over nightly by busloads of hippies, surfers and other visitors wanting to sleep four to a room for fifteen bucks a pop. The center of the lodge was the two-room compound that served as a combination kitchen and dining room and nightclub. There was a long table and a dozen chairs and a couple of battered couches and a pool table in the far corner and an old television showing surf films with the sound always switched off and a stereo that was always switched on.

On the southern edge of the property, the Youngs had con-
structed a broad-beamed wooden A-frame that overlooked a swatch
of Maori land that nestled the first of Raglan's fabled points, a
surfbreak known as Indicators. There were wood floors and high
ceilings and deep fireplaces and an upstairs bedroom reached by a
curving staircase, the banister smooth and elegant, custom-made by
a local shipbuilder. The place felt more like a ski chalet than a
beach house, except for the surfboards that hung on all walls.
Many were collector's items, among those the original Bear board
from the film *Big Wednesday,* arguably the most famous surfboard
of all.

Big Wednesday is a surfer's film more than a surf film. It tells the
story of three local wave riders, played by Gary Busey, Jan-Michael
Vincent and William Katt, caught in the rude trajectory that was
the Vietnam era. It's a coming-of-age story of problem marriages,
problem wars and problem drinkers; of friendship and hardship,
and of how the former may be the only known antidote for the
latter. In the movie, Sam Melville plays Bear: spiritual guru, surf
elder, board shaper, the living embodiment of the sport's old ways
and the man who prophesizes "a swell so big it will wipe everything that came before it." A line that is both the surfer's version of
the *Taxi Driver* favorite—"someday a real rain will come and wash
all this scum from the streets"—and a much more interesting
proposition altogether.

Two Bear boards were shaped for the film; one was later de-
stroyed, the other given to Jan-Michael Vincent. As is fitting for
stories such as these, but inconvenient otherwise, the character
Vincent played in *Big Wednesday,* much like the character Vincent
played in real life, was a bright star ascended too early, a young
pup cold-plunged into the heaven of fame and the hell of addiction. The booze and the drugs cost money and more money, and
eventually Vincent found himself on the wanting, supply side of

114

this familiar economic theory. He sold the Bear board to his agent, Dave Wirtschafter, something of a Hollywood legend and the current president of the William Morris Agency. Considering the circumstances, I imagine this transaction was made for cash and not credit. Wirtschafter had worked with Vincent but had grown up with Charlie and sometime later, when his friend decided to move to New Zealand, threw him a party and gave him the Bear board as a good-bye present.

"Man, that was some party," Charlie told me, by way of explanation. He told me this while standing in the kitchen of the main compound, peeling potatoes with a practiced hand. There were fifty of them, stacked haphazardly on the counter in front of him. It was strange to be in New Zealand hearing stories of people from home, but stranger still to find one of surfing's totem objects sitting in a house on a bluff overlooking the point at Raglan. It seemed to be an omen, good or otherwise, so we checked in for the night.

24

We'd slept in the Bird's Nest, a two-story slat-wood bungalow perched atop a steep hill, and awoke to find the next day bright and blue. From the upstairs porch, the take-off spot at the first of Raglan's three points was barely visible. The view improved if you stood atop the wooden railing that rimmed the porch. On the other side of that railing was a forty-foot drop, but that seemed to be part of the experience, so I stood there and drank a cup of coffee and watched waves wrap into the bay. We were a mile from the beach, maybe farther, but those waves didn't look small.

Downstairs, I could hear the Johns debating boards. They had each brought a shortboard and a gun, while I had a shortboard and a funboard. To understand the nature of their debate, you need to understand a bit about varieties of surfboards. Longboards, the classic cars of the sport, are stately and slow and often difficult to handle when the waves get big and steep. Because surfers wanted a shot at more difficult surf, guns evolved from longboards. For speed, guns have a narrower frame and a pointed nose and tail; for speed is of the essence when riding big waves. Shortboards arrived in the seventies, when the desire for maneuverability dropped board sizes from ten feet to seven, a design feature that birthed all the shenanigans that make modern surfing appear an acrobatic circus. In the years since, they have shrunk further still, now running into the much-abridged five foot range. These days, my six-six shortboard is only considered a shortboard for guys much bigger than me, on the plus side of six feet and two hundred pounds. On the other hand, a funboard sits halfway between both extremes, offering more maneuverability than a longboard and more floatation than a shortboard. It is the happy medium of mediocrity. Funboard riders either have nothing left to prove or lack the skills to prove anything.

That day I should have brought my funboard, but the Johns were going small and, ego being what it was, I followed their lead and threw my shortboard in the car. When we got to the beach, there were thirty cars in the parking lot and sixty guys in the water. The waves were overhead, thick and cold. As I put on my wetsuit, I watched locals take off so deep in the pit—one wrong slip—but these guys weren't slipping. I looked around for the Johns but realized they had already headed out into the water.

I was alone in the parking lot with no real idea where to paddle out. As far as I could tell, there were two choices: paddle safely around the point, easily a fifteen-minute proposition, or scramble over a long boulder field and find a tall rock and jump. Jumping was all about timing. From the top of the rock, you had to wait for the last wave in a big set to crash, dive into its foam and paddle like mad. Some surfers made it to the lineup with their hair dry; others were slammed onto the rocks. I wanted to make the smart decision but saw no one paddling around the point and wasn't sure where it was best to get in the water. I thought about jumping off the rocks, but which were the right rocks? The beach was lined with boulders. I spotted another surfer in the parking lot, wetsuit already zipped, board already waxed. He looked local. Rather than asking if he was local or if he knew the right way to jump off the rocks or, for that matter, if he could save me the trouble and just bounce up and down on my head for a while, I decided to follow him out.

He walked down to the southern part of the beach and started picking his way across the boulders. They were slippery and wet and covered with the kinds of sharp edges that made walking difficult and falling dangerous. He was a few steps ahead of me when we reached the edge of the water, and I stopped to watch as he climbed up on a small boulder, steadied himself and leaped when the next wave arrived. There was another wave behind it, but he dove through it without a problem. I hopped onto the same boulder he had jumped from, but didn't have time to get my balance. The foam from that last wave crashed and hit my ankles with more force than I was expecting. I lost my footing and pitched forward and ended up on my belly on my board with nothing to do but paddle like hell. A few strokes out, the current caught me. It was too strong and running the wrong way down the beach, and my shortboard didn't paddle as quickly as my funboard. I had gone barely thirty feet when the first wave of the next set appeared.

There's an art to duck diving, one with which I am not too familiar. I took a deep breath and shoved the nose of my board underwater and got my foot on the back and pressed the tail down. The goal was to get body and board down beneath that wave, letting it roll harmlessly over me but I hadn't sunk deep enough and the whitewater grabbed my shoulders and I lost ground fast. I got free and managed a dozen strokes forward when the next wave appeared, bigger than the last. I tried to dive through it and popped up and saw another, and this one was more serious still.

I tried to paddle over it but got caught at the last second and sucked up the face as the lip started to pitch, and was flipped onto my back and hurled over the falls. There was a dull roar, a stinging in my sinuses. I was underwater for a second when the wave's lip landed. It smashed straight into my chest. The air was smacked from my lungs, and I went pinballing around underwater. There were hard objects everywhere. I covered my head; something hit my hip—a rock or my board—no way to know for sure. I started to swim for the surface but had no idea which direction was up. I looked around and finally saw a spot of sunlight and swam for it. There was enough time for one gulp of air before the next wave landed.

In surfing, no matter what happens out there, you can usually turn around and swim in. Surfers get into trouble because they persist in losing battles. In almost every situation you can retreat and live to fight another day. In almost every situation, except when paddling in means paddling straight onto the rocks. Paddling onto the rocks means uncertain consequences and I knew what kinds of uncertain consequences surfing could bring.

Years back, on another bright and blue day, I'd been surfing about ten miles south of San Francisco, at a beginner break or as much of a beginner break as can be found in San Francisco. That day, I had been surfing the northern end of the beach when I noticed people crowding around the southern end. I didn't pay much attention until an ambulance drove onto the sand. By the time I got out of the water, there was a boy, not much past fifteen, lying on a stretcher. The paramedics were moving slowly, their heads hanging down. I watched a girl sob to her knees. By the time I arrived, they had covered him with a sheet. He had snapped his neck riding the shorebreak and was dead before anyone even got him out of the water. The paramedics, the sobbing girl, the white sheet, everything I was seeing was just final formality.

That Raglan day, there were no formalities. I didn't have the strength to fight the waves so I paddled onto the rocks. The rocks took a small chunk of my board, a larger chunk of my shin. By the time I caught my breath, I was utterly spent. It was mainly adrenaline, mainly fear. Even the rock bashing I had taken was no worse than many others. It was a bit of a deal, but not a big one.

Afterward, I walked down the beach and tried to paddle around the point. My left ankle hurt, and later I would find a bruise shaped like a kidney just below my calf. I was too jumpy, and my strokes were off. Every time I saw a wave, I started steering away from it, ending up way outside the lineup. It took forever to make it into position, and when I did I was already too tired. My heart wasn't in it. It started to rain, a cold drizzle. Even in my winter wetsuit I was shivering. Two hours I stuck it out but never caught a wave.

I trudged up onto the shore and into the parking lot, and the temperature dropped ten degrees, and I realized that one of the Johns had the keys to the van. The last I had seen of them was out in water, picking off waves that I was too cold and too tired and too scared even to consider. I sat down to wait, and the rain came down harder, and a heavy fog began to creep in. Eventually, the Johns showed up and mentioned that the swell was not supposed to last through the afternoon. The forecast said this side of the island would get no more waves anytime soon. They were talking about other possible destinations as we pulled out of the parking lot. By then the fog was so thick that I couldn't even get a last look at the wave I had traveled halfway around the world to surf.

25

That night, we stood around the Karioi Lodge and waited for dinner to be ready. It was Easter vacation. Australian college students had been arriving all afternoon. They were mainly young women, traveling in some semblance of a guided tour. They wore jeans, tank tops, little makeup, the odd puka shell necklace. The room filled with their nasal birdsong. In the kitchen, Charlie Young was cooking lamb for fifty. Outside, the rain was still falling, and the grill, which was set up at the edge of the porch, caught errant droplets. The meat hissed and sputtered, and everyone got drunk on cheap beer.

For two days, I'd been looking for a chance to talk to Charlie about the Conductor but could never seem to get him away from the pack of locals who trailed him at all times. They were a motley crew who had long grown used to the lodge's endless stream of visitors and viewed all with a predatory disinterest. From experience, I knew few people were comfortable talking about the mystical in public and fewer still in a nuts-and-bolts place like New Zealand. Already, there had been incidents:

"What are you doing in New Zealand?"

"I'm looking into this story I heard about a surfer called the Conductor."

"Who's the Conductor?"

"It's a legend, really, about a surfer who could control the weather."

"Surfers can't control the weather."

"Well, no shit. It's a legend, a myth, I'm just interested in where it came from. There's all this magic in the story, and I want to know why there's all this magic in a surf story."

"What the hell for—are you from California?"

I've found that the level of animosity the Conductor produces seems inversely proportional to the number of people around when I start asking questions. The times I'd been forced into telling the Conductor's story to a large group, it was met with cold stares and awkward silences and the now familiar rejoinder: surfers can't control the weather. It didn't matter that I might have shared that opinion. What mattered was that by telling the story and asking the question I'd nudged too close to the world of spiritual beliefs and surfing's relationship to such beliefs, and by doing so publicly I'd broken some small taboo, crossed a mostly unnoticed line. For these reasons, I was hoping to get a few minutes alone with Charlie, but it wasn't going to happen anytime soon.

Instead I passed the time talking surf spots with the driver who manned the tour bus that had brought most of the Australians. He was tough and old and odd. His brown hair looked dyed, most likely wasn't. His skin fit him like an old shirt. He was a talker, but not a friendly one. There was an unspoken hint of violence beneath his words. Something might set him off; it was hard to determine what.

We stood toward one side of the living room, where a map of New Zealand had been tacked to the wall. He pointed out secret breaks, places he had scored perfect tubes in his youth, places he wanted to return to temporally more than geographically. He paused and looked thoughtfully at his country, finally tapping a spot in the far north.

"Good surf here, but you got to ask permission."

"Permission?"

"Maori. Permission to cross their land. No big deal. They'll either say yes or no. All you have to do is drive up to the gate. They'll be twenty people in the front yard; most of them will be holding axes. You never know, though, might be worth it. Good surf here."

With no swell on the horizon, the Johns had been thinking about heading to the Mahia Peninsula.

"You've got to be careful there," he said.

"At Mahia?"

"I surfed a lot in my teens and early twenties, then put it away and worked like a dog till I was thirty. Made some money, didn't like the life. I fucked off and surfed through my thirties and forties. Now I'm a fifty-four-year-old bus driver. A bus driver. You've got to be careful."

26

After dinner I was sitting on the porch drinking beer and talking about the Conductor with a couple of Dutch guys and a couple of Dutch girls, all here on vacation, when the John who was the friend of my friend John ambled over. He was among those who thought my story strict hogwash and expressed his displeasure by interrupting our chat with a tale all his own. There's a sordid underside to surf culture, and John had been a part of it. He recounted a surf trip through Central America when he hadn't done much wave riding but had managed to spend a bit of time smoking crack in a whorehouse in Costa Rica. He bought his rocks from the madam and then smoked them in a dirty broom closet with a bare mattress squeezed on the floor, his company for this adventure an ugly hooker rentable by the hour. That the ugly hooker turned out to be fourteen years old and the madam's daughter didn't make the story any easier to listen to. No one much felt like talking when he had finished. I got up and walked inside to see if I could talk to Charlie Young about the Conductor, but Charlie Young knew nothing of the Conductor.

"I've heard plenty of surf stories," he told me. "I've never heard one like that."

We were standing in the kitchen, dinner finished, dishes piled in a dirty stack in a large sink. Three big aluminum pails stood in a corner, collecting recycling, compost and garbage respectively. Behind the pails stood a long table, and on it sat three locals, somewhere between boys and men, sharing a bottle of beer.

"You ever heard anything like that?" Charlie asked them.

No one said anything. No one could be bothered.

It was the same reluctance I had encountered elsewhere, and it was a reluctance that followed a larger pattern.

27

Scholars use the words *logos* and *mythos* to describe the two main ways humans evolved to arrive at knowledge. *Logos,* meaning "logic," is information of the no-nonsense variety: practical, clinical, scientific, secular. It is a way of thinking that helps us function best in society. In the world of logos, it doesn't matter that fire was a gift from the gods; what matters is that fire is hot and you don't want to stick your hand into it. Where this becomes difficult is when that same fire gets out of control and burns down a village. In the face of such sweeping tragedy, a larger context is often desired, but the cold calculus of logos—fire burns hot—merely leaves survivors befuddled. This used to be where mythos came in.

Mythos was a way of giving meaning to events that existed beyond easy context. For good reason, all of history's fantastic stories—from biblical tales to Maori myths—fall into this category. Mythos was a way of reminding people that life's point was spiritual, eternal, deeper, greater, whatever. This fact may explain why the need for mythos stretches across cultural boundaries. Scientists got their first inkling of mythological omnipresence in the latter half of the eighteenth century, when the German anthropologist Adolph Bastian made a global study of such stories and noticed that they all seem to be built on the same core ideas. The psychiatrist Carl Jung named these core ideas *archetypes* and extended Bastian's work by arguing that archetypes were not only the building blocks of an individual's unconscious mind but also the cornerstone of a shared *collective unconscious,* a slippery term he defined as a "storehouse of latent memory traces inherited from man's ancestral past." Later he broadened that ancestral past beyond the border of species, into our "pre-human or animal ancestry as well."

Jung reached his conclusions after completing a worldwide study of dreams and noticing that no matter where on the planet he was or whose dreams he was examining, the same symbols kept cropping up. Oftentimes, these symbols meant little to the dreamer but still carried an enormous emotional charge. Examining the symbols categorically, Jung found that most represented broad, cross-cultural mythological concepts, such as *father* or *mother* or *shadow* or *hero*. The reason for this, he came to believe, was that these archetypes were hardwired into our genes. He thought this could explain why myths and dreams and odd encounters and less-than-random coincidences always caught our attention; they were examples of the collective unconscious trying to get our attention. It wasn't just that these things felt important; they were important.

In his 1949 *The Hero with a 1000 Faces,* Joseph Campbell took matters one step further, arguing that all of humankind's stories are actually one story, named *the hero's journey* and summarized with the adage "All religions are true, but none are literal." But in the past three hundred years, we have forgotten this adage. From the Industrial Revolution forward, as humankind got better and better at science, mythos—as a functioning rubric—lost its luster. As the former nun and religious scholar Karen Armstrong writes in her account of the rise of fundamentalism, *The Battle for God*:

> In the pre-modern world, both mythos and logos were regarded as indispensable. Each would be impoverished without the other . . . By the eighteenth century, however, the people of Europe and America had achieved such

astonishing success in science and technology that they began to think that *logos* was the only means to truth and began to discount *mythos* as false and superstitious. It is also true that the new world they were creating contradicted the old mythical spirituality. Our religious experience in the modern world has changed, and because an increasing number of people regard scientific rationalism alone as true, they have often tried to turn the mythos of their faith into logos.

Armstrong's point is that rationalism shamed mythos out of sight. In its wake, new logocentric ideas—like scientific secularism and fundamentalist inerrancy—arose to fill the vacuum. But one of the interesting by-products of this rise was that the so-called soft sciences, fields like psychology and anthropology, where the study of myth seems crucial, began looking for ways to become harder. Scientists who once looked at mythos as a representation of our inner world, began distrusting the validity of that inner world. Subjectivity was out; objectivity came next.

Among those who turned this way was Claude Lévi-Strauss. Trained as a philosopher, in the 1930s, Lévi-Strauss switched to anthropology because he was interested in a more rigorous approach to facts. His early work involved a worldwide study of marriage customs. Lévi-Strauss reasoned that if marriage customs were strictly cultural, they would be ultimately arbitrary, varying from place to place and from society to society. But he discovered the exact opposite. In every culture he examined he found certain fundamental ideas surrounding marriage repeated themselves, with the prohibition against incest being first and foremost.

Sir James Frazer had been the first to demonstrate the universality of the incest taboo in his 1910 study *Totemism and Exogamy*. Sigmund Freud soon added to the idea in *Totem and Taboo,* arguing that the totems and taboos of tribal religions were the product of primitive peoples projecting the contents of their mostly primitive minds onto the real world. "The projection of their own evil impulses into demons is only one portion of the *Weltanschauung* [worldview] of primitive peoples, and which we shall come to know as 'animism.'" Much of that work focused on the aborigines of Australia, who practiced *exogamy*—marriage outside of the immediate tribe—which Freud linked to the incest taboo and later extended into his famous Oedipus complex. But it was Lévi-Strauss who further elevated the incest taboo from one of the basic components of our subconscious minds to the "fundamental step because of which, by which, but above all in which, the transition from nature to culture is accomplished."

To this end, he called the incest taboo a *deep structure,* unvarying and ubiquitous. The reason for this was simply that incest is bad for the gene pool. Sleep with your brothers and sisters, and pretty soon mutations arise. If that pattern of intimate relations with intimate relations continues for more than a few generations, pregnancy becomes impossible. The line dies out. Incest isn't just a cultural taboo; it's a biological taboo. More than that, Lévi-Strauss realized the prohibition forced us to breed outside the nest, and this comingling of families provided society with its most basic building blocks. For these reasons, much like the linguist Noam Chomsky's universal grammar, Lévi-Strauss thought these deep structures were hardwired into our brain. He deduced that we are a species of mythologists because our myths contain the rules for our survival.

In the seventies, the ethnologist Charles Laughlin and the neurology-trained psychiatrist and anthropologist Eugene D'Aquili began looking for ways to marry Lévi-Strauss's structuralist anthropology with what had since been learned from evolutionary theory. One of the first things they set out to do was tear down the theoretical wall that existed between humans and animals, realizing that if the need for myth was coded into human brains, its vestiges must be present in the lower orders as well. Since questioning the animal kingdom about why it did certain things proved problematic, they instead chose to study the pattern of behavior that surrounded those things known as ritual.

In nature, they found, ritual is everywhere. Whales breech; peacocks display; bees dance. From a biological perspective, Laughlin and D'Aquili wanted to know what purpose all of this serves. Evolutionary theory teaches us that the brain's primary function is to keep an organism alive and reproducing, and, in turn, everything from love to hunger is fundamentally an expression of this primary function. The proximity of a viable sexual partner produces lust, much in the way that a shortage of glucose in the bloodstream produces hunger. Sex and eating, by satisfying these needs, produce an accompanying pleasure response. Without this response, we would stop mating and stop eating.

Laughlin and D'Aquili reasoned that as our brain evolved, this chain of command lengthened. Eating became associated with cooking, which became associated with hunting and so forth. In this chain of association, it wasn't just the action of eating that produced pleasure; it was the ritual surrounding eating that produced pleasure. The reasoning behind this ritual was that, as our species evolved and grew in size, our nutritional needs grew alongside us. No longer could we anchor ourselves to a rock like a barnacle and feed on whatever floated by. If a wolf only ate the animals that wandered into its mouth, it would be dead within a week. To sustain all that body mass, wolves had to figure out how to hunt. And it was wolves that Laughlin and D'Aquili decided to study.

In 1979, they published *The Spectrum of Ritual,* outlining their basic ideas. Before hunting, wolves go through a ceremonial tail-wagging, group-howling session. Since wolves often hunt animals considerably larger than themselves, a level of coordination ensures both a greater chance of success and a minimization of danger. This ceremonial tail-wagging, group-howling session—based on an outgrowth of the exact same need/response pattern—establishes order and rank for the coming battle. From this, Laughlin and D'Aquili deduced that ritual serves two important biological functions: it coordinates the brain to allow for group action, and it teaches the young how to behave. This is why ritual is found everywhere in nature, because it is part of the engine that drives nature forward. But this explanation leaves one critical question unanswered: in humans, why did ritual become intertwined with myth?

The psychologist Frederic Bartlett was the first to realize that memory creates patterns in our brain. These patterns, which he called *schemas,* provide the mental framework for understanding and remembering information. The most basic schema is found when humans encounter something they don't recognize. Since the drive to procreate is among our most fundamental, the question we always ask when encountering the unknown is "is this thing like me or not like me?" The reason we ask is obvious: if this new thing is like me, maybe I can breed with it; if it's not like me, maybe I should run away from it.

But as humans evolved, the things they encountered grew in number. They started asking more questions and developing more and more schemas. One of those other schemas was the need to know why something happened. Laughlin and D'Aquili argued that this need developed into a "cognitive imperative." By helping us to quickly adapt to our environment, this imperative contributes much to our success. But humans often encounter illness, death, odd coincidences, mysterious occurrences—things that do not allow for easy understanding. Yet evolution designed the human brain to detect meaning, and this mechanism doesn't just shut down when easy answers aren't readily forthcoming. Hence the need to invent meaning—gods, demons, supernatural forces—is based on an automatic process. Mythos is how humankind resolves the irresolvable. But because we adapt physically as well as mentally, ritualized action has become associated with mythologized meaning. And biologically, people who are better-functioning members of society have a better chance at passing on their genes, meaning this tendency toward myth and ritual was a trait selected as part of what helped the fittest survive. Steven Pinker, author and director of MIT's Center for Cognitive Biology, summarizes this nicely when he says, "Religion is a technique for success."

But, as Armstrong noted, the modern world is bereft of traditional mythologies, and since our need for myth is part of our fundamental biology—somehow tied both to the immune system and to our neurochemistry—we are, as such, shorting out our body's need/reward system. When myth is denied to us in customary forms—since humans don't much enjoy suffering—we look for new sources. Nowadays those sources are often found in fiction, poetry, cinema, sports, television, but this is myth at a distance. And myth at a distance, as Daniel Pinchbeck points out in his excellent *Breaking Open the Head,* is not without certain consequences.

Modernism caused a profound shift in the way we use our senses. In his book *Myth and Meaning,* Lévi-Strauss admitted his initial shock when he discovered Indian tribesman were able to see the planet Venus in daylight, with the naked eye—"something that to me would be utterly impossible and incredible." But he learned from astronomers that it was feasible, and he found ancient accounts of Western navigators with the ability. "Today we use less and we use more of our mental capacity than we did in the past," he realized. We have sacrificed perceptual capabilities for other mental abilities—to concentrate on a computer screen while sitting in a cubicle for many hours at a stretch (something those

Indians would find "utterly impossible and incredible"), or to shut off multiple levels of awareness as we drive a car in heavy traffic. In other words, we are brought up within a system that teaches us to postpone, defer, and eliminate most incoming sense data in favor of a future reward. We live in a feedback loop of perpetual postponement. For the most part, we are not even aware of what we have lost.

On average the human brain takes in 400 billion bits of information a second, but only two thousand of those bits make it up to our consciousness. Those two thousand bits, at least for most of us, represent the end limit of our processing capacity. When Lévi-Strauss writes that "today we use less and we use more of our mental capacity than we did in the past," what he means is we now process two thousand different bits of information a second than we did in the past. Part of this is straightforward use it or lose it atrophy and some of this happens because, as research done by Eric Kandel at Columbia University and Candice Pert at Georgetown University proved down to the molecular level, our emotions help regulate our perceptions. Pert, one of the chief scientists responsible for our understanding of the brain's chemistry and, by extension, almost everything we think of when we think of modern neuroscience, explains how this works in her book *Molecules of Emotion.*

Emotions are constantly regulating what we experience as "reality." The decision about what sensory information travels to your brain and what gets filtered out depends on what signals the receptors are receiving from peptides. [Pert calls peptides "the molecules of emotion."] There is a plethora of elegant neurophysiological data suggesting that the nervous system is not capable of taking in everything, but can only scan the outer world for material that it is prepared to find by virtue of its wiring hook ups, its own internal patterns, and its past experience.

This means, at least on some level, what we believe governs what we see—though nobody is yet certain how much or how little of this is going on. Which means that belief governs perception, which shapes reality or, as some consciousness researchers now believe, is synonymous with reality and thus our reality—what we think of as the real world—is nothing, quite literally, beyond what we believe. It raises the question: what kind of effect does this have on our version of reality when a society stops believing in the mythological?

Charlie Young and the rest of the surfers sitting around that kitchen were not just reluctant to discuss the Conductor; they were reluctant even to discuss the possibility of the Conductor. If all of these scientists are correct, it wasn't that these surfers had never heard the story; it was that what they believed about the nature of reality actually limited their ability to hear the story—as if things weren't weird enough already.

PART FOUR

He went to the river. The river was there.

—Ernest Hemingway

PART FOUR

28

Polynesians first arrived in what is now the town of Gisborne, on the East Coast of New Zealand's North Island, almost seven hundred years ago. In the intervening centuries, they settled and went native, farming and fishing and fighting just about anything and everything they could. In 1769, Captain James Cook tried to replenish his stocks from nearby shores and met such Maori hostility that he decided not to bother. He left wanting and hungry, though Gisborne's wide-mouthed inlet still bears his moniker—Poverty Bay—as a reminder of these troubles.

It's the type of place where the residents take a small bit of pride in being from Poverty Bay, either because they're tough enough not to mind or already in on the joke. As a reward, perhaps, both Poverty Bay and the town of Gisborne are the first places on Earth to see the sun rise. This daily greeting is so auspicious that on January 1, at the turn of the last millennium, a hundred thousand people came to this town to celebrate new day's dawning.

A couple of years after that, on the day the Johns and I left Raglan and drove across the island to chase the surf to Gisborne, no hint of that party remained. Instead we found an empty stretch of buildings, forgotten and dusty, a windswept locale like the Texas of Peter Bogdanovich's film *The Last Picture Show*. This may have had more to do with the fact that we first drove down the main drag on Easter Sunday, when everyone was at home or church or, at least,

elsewhere. The movie theater looked empty and forbidden. Surrounding the theater was a long row of stores and restaurants, but
those too were shuttered tight for the holiday. The only people out
were a smash of teenagers on skateboards and an assortment of
tourists, walking alone or in quiet pairs. It was as far from a beach
town as any I've ever seen.

It was nearing sunset by the time we drove through town, but
none of us wanted to stop. After the long car ride, we needed
nothing more than a little exercise. The beach was somewhere
nearby, at least according to the map. Our surfer's guidebook was
of little help, so we drove until we found a coastal road and then
drove that coastal road until we saw another car carrying surfboards on its roof. We turned into a tiny dirt parking lot; a nearby
sign read: WAINUI BEACH.

The car we followed had parked, doors had opened, and a trio
of teenagers had climbed out. They were stocky and silent and serious, surveying the waves with arms crossed and caps pulled low.
The wind was up, and the surf looked terrible. The teenagers left as
quickly as they came, and the Johns were thinking of doing the
same, but I was still smarting from the beating I had taken at
Raglan the previous day, and deeply in need of a shot at redemption. I went to change before anyone could talk me out of it.

It didn't take long for me to get my shot. As we were paddling
out, the wind died, the ocean got glassy and the waves began pouring in, clean and rideable. Bigger sets started to arrive. I watched
one of the Johns spin his board and pick off a perfect, shoulder-
high, left peeler, dropping down beneath the curl, a slowly vanishing shadow sailing gleefully down the beach. I paddled fast to my
left, angling toward the next wave, stroked and stood and felt the
board accelerate and pumped once and into my bottom turn, and
then the world vanished. There was no self, no other. For an instant,

I didn't know where I ended and the wave began. This was an instant beyond the redemption I had hoped to find.

Surfing is a game of such instants. The Japanese use the word *aware* to mean "transitory beauty," describing things that are staggeringly impactful and simultaneously vanishing. There are dozens of surf terms that all fail at capturing this moment. Longboarders, especially older ones, use *the glide* to mean "the psychotropic effect of nose-riding." Tube hunters speak of being in *the green room,* which technically connotes the inside of a barrel, but truthfully refers to the feeling of being utterly, finally, fleetingly, awake.

Mihaly Csikszentmihalyi, a former University of Chicago psychologist and department chairman, has made a career out of studying such instants. In research done in the past three decades, he found they exist not only in surfing or solely in athletics, but also in activities as wide-ranging as painting and chess playing and heart surgery. To describe such moments, athletes often use the term *in the zone,* while psychologists prefer *flow state.* Csikszentmihalyi defines this state as "being so involved in an activity that nothing else seems to matter: The ego falls away. Time flies. Every action, movement and thought follows inevitably from the previous one, like playing jazz. Your whole being is involved, and you're using your skills to the utmost." He has found that the experience itself is so enjoyable that people will do it even at great cost, for the sheer sake of doing it. When people are entrenched in such a state, as Csikszentmihalyi points out in his book *Flow,* "they stop being aware of themselves as separate from the actions they are performing." In other words, time and space vanish, self vanishes and the now swallows us whole.

If this sounds similar to the phrasing often used to describe so-called spiritual experiences that is not without reason. In the years since Csikszentmihalyi did his research, scientists looking further into flow states and their relationship to spirituality have begun utilizing more advanced personality profiles like the Temperament and Character Inventory created by Robert Cloninger, a psychiatrist at the University of Washington. Cloninger's TCI is one of the most widely respected and often utilized personality profiles, designed to consider not simply the psychological factors of personality but social, environmental, biological and neurochemical components as well. It comes at personality profiling with a mathematical rigor that had long been missing from traditional psychological testing. The TCI was also one of the first personality profiles to measure a trait known as *self-transcendence*. The term is used to describe spiritual feelings that are independent of traditional religiosity. The National Institutes of Health geneticist Dean Hamer describes this trait in his book *The God Gene* as

> not based on belief in particular God, frequency of prayer, or other orthodox religious doctrines or practices. Instead, it gets to the heart of spiritual belief: the nature of the universe and our place in it. Self-transcendent individuals tend to see everything, including themselves, as part of a great totality. They have a strong sense of "at-one-ness"— of the connections between people, places and things. Non-self-transcendent people, on the other hand, tend to have a more self-centered viewpoint. They focus on differences and discrepancies between people, places and things, rather than similarities and interrelationships.

Self-transcendence is composed of three distinct but related components. The first two components are known as *transpersonal identification* and *mysticism,* with transpersonal identification being a form of empathy writ large. It's a willingness to identify not just with fellow humans but with plants and animals and even the planet itself. Mysticism is pretty much what it sounds like: a measure of one's willingness to be interested in things that cannot be explained by rationale and reason. The third component, and possibly the most important, is known as *self-forgetfulness*. Those of us who are more self-forgetful have an easier time getting lost in the moment, being absorbed in art and music and sport, in achieving Csikszentmihalyi's flow state.

These three components have been found to hang together; that is, someone who scores high for one trait will usually score high for the others as well. "In other words," writes Hamer, "self-transcendence is as distinct from other parts of the personality as eye and hair coloration are from size."

This becomes increasingly interesting when the relationship between such self-transcendent spirituality and health is examined. From a biological perspective, scientists are now beginning to suspect that self-transcendence may be a rather helpful trait. In the past few decades, hundreds of studies done by hundreds of researchers have shown that spiritual people live longer and have healthier lives than nonspiritual people. Studies have proven that some kind of participatory faith lowers the risk for drug addiction, suicide, cancer, high blood pressure, stress, stroke, heart disease and dozens of other serious ailments. So many of these studies have now been done that in the past five years researchers have begun doing meta-studies of them. One of these, conducted by the Mayo Clinic in 2001, reviewed nearly 350 studies of physical health and 850 studies of mental health, all of which used religious and spiritual variables. When they analyzed their data, the Mayo researchers found that spirituality was consistently associated with "better health outcomes," while eighteen recent longevity studies showed that those spiritually inclined lived up to 30 percent longer than atheists. For years, these health benefits have been attributed to socioeconomic, environmental and psychological factors, but a number of these metaanalyses have been designed to remove all of these elements and still the outcomes stay the same. In plainer terms, as Dr. Harold Koenig of Duke University Medical Center recently pointed out to the *New Republic*, "Lack of religious involvement has an effect on mortality that is equivalent to forty years of smoking one pack of cigarettes a day."

29

That day in Gisborne, the Johns and I rode waves until the sun went down, reluctantly climbing out of the water when the sky turned a deep purple. It was a great session, and afterward we violated the sport's cardinal rule—never leave good surf—and instead changed out of our wetsuits and lit out south, driving thin roads the length of Poverty Bay as the sky above us grew dark and dizzy with stars. We passed through the Wharerata Forest, and drove farther still, heading to the edge of the Mahia Peninsula. We had heard about a campground there but found a dirt-packed lot, nearly treeless, thick with RVs. It smelled wrong, felt worse. It was like Mr. Rogers's Neighborhood if Mr. Rogers had been a three-pack-a-day smoker with a meth lab in his bathtub. The whole area had been tuned to the wrong frequency, all ill winds and bad vibes. No one felt like cooking. We ate dry crackers and old cheese, spent twenty minutes figuring out how to keep all of our surfboards locked inside the van and went to bed among them.

The van was a Maui Cruiser and looked like the bastard child of a Volkswagen Microbus and R2-D2, but larger and more uncomfortable. I took the roof bunk, a space maybe ten inches high. Getting up there required dicey gymnastics and getting down took lubricant. When I was four years old, I bashed my eyebrow into a coffee table and required stitches. The doctors used a heavyweight lead blanket to pin me in place, and I have been severely claustrophobic ever since. The next morning we were all up early.

In daylight, there was even less to recommend about the campground. Some of our neighboring RVs looked rusted to the ground. Trash barrels brimmed with beer cans; laundry flapped from makeshift lines. There was a little cantina, over by the main gates, and since no one wanted to stick around long enough to fire up the stove, I went searching for coffee.

Instead, I found two women, neither much older than twenty-five, standing beside the cantina's locked door. They had laundry baskets piled high with dirty clothes and a sore need for quarters. Their names were Lizzy and Audrey, and they lived in Auckland, doing as little as they could, or at least that's what they told me. They had taken their kids camping because their husbands had the week off and had gone to Australia, possibly Thailand.

"They're someplace," said Lizzy.

"Yeah, someplace where the pussy's younger," said Audrey.

I looked over at the cantina. A sign by the door said it would be another fifteen minutes until the shop opened and probably longer until someone got around to making coffee. Lizzy lit up a cigarette and mentioned their intention to wait it out. "Like where the fuck am I gonna go?" No one needed coffee that badly. I left them there, heading off to check the surf.

The Mahia Peninsula used to be a separate island but now forms the country's largest tombolo, dangling off the East Coast like a lopsided diamond. Its southern flanks face open ocean, and when the big storms churn across the South Pacific, their brute force reaches Mahia's beaches unhindered. Very few people live there, and the ones who do have been packed into a cluster of windswept saltboxes not far from the campground. Beyond those were penny-ante farms and the odd roadside mom-and-pop, but mainly the land was big and rugged and empty.

In our hunt, we drove nearly every inch: seaside highways, tiny mountainside cow tracks, hours and hours with mainly sheep for company. Our engine whined through the uphill stretches, and no guardrail protected the down. Often we rounded hairpin corners where the outer edge of the track gave way to high cliffs and vertiginous views and the constant threat of bad endings.

From a number of such spots we could see both coasts simultaneously, and, for our needs, both had their problems. The wind was bashing hard on one side; the other had no waves. But we were stubborn, taking all morning to verify the blatantly obvious. We'd gotten out of the car on four occasions to hike hills and round bends and follow paths that might or might not have been the right way. We checked Blacks and Last Chance and The Spit. The Johns ached for a whirling right that crashed over a nearly disintegrated breakwall and looked fully deserving of its name: Annihilation. By early afternoon we were on each other's nerves. There were no good choices, so we settled for Mahanga Beach, near the entrance to the peninsula, paddling out for lazy ripples mostly too small and too slow to push even the longest of longboards.

"Man, if the wind would just die down."

"Or the swell pick up."

"Or if we hadn't left Gisborne."

In the end we drove back to Gisborne, back to the same parking lot on Wainui Beach, hoping for another late afternoon session, instead finding the wind up and serious about staying that way. Yesterday's teenagers were nowhere in sight, but we met a woman there. She was in her early thirties, busty and tall, with long black hair, tight jeans, a pink sweatshirt and a denim jacket, and rock-star sunglasses covering half of her face. She gazed at the surf from a tiny hummock and looked like a high-concept hood ornament sold only in Japan.

We stood beside her, but it was only a gesture. The ocean was a soup pot on full boil.

145

"You should have been here this morning," said the woman. "Head high, offshore winds, perfect barrels."

One of the things that sets a surf quest apart from nearly all other such crusades is that sooner or later, given enough time and enough effort, you will actually find the omnipresent perfection in nature of great waves. The surf quest is one of the only places where the laws of physics—especially as they pertain to lunar gravity and its effects on large liquid bodies—and the promise of the mystical so clearly bisect. That said, when she told us we had missed our shot at an epic session, we took it like men: we swore in several languages and scuffed our shoes.

"You never know," she said. "It could clean up."

Kiwis, as a rule, are ridiculously optimistic. There seems to be an unspoken national agreement to say nice things, despite their manifest impossibility. The waves would come back and the surf would be the greatest ever. If not now, then soon; if not soon, then tomorrow; if not tomorrow morning, then certainly by early afternoon. We had been in country for over a week, and the one thing that was absolute was that the winds never died in the early afternoon, but that didn't seem to matter. In American culture, the best we can offer is our ability to make a dollar out of two dimes; in New Zealand their best is not to notice the two dimes and to spend them like they were really a dollar.

"It'll definitely be better tomorrow," she said.

30

Her name was Françoise Lewis and she really thought the surf would be better tomorrow, and we really wanted to believe her. So we took her advice and followed her down the road to a freshly painted, two-story Victorian with an upstairs balcony, that afforded a tremendous view of the ocean. This was the Chalet Surf Lodge, another of New Zealand's backpacker's accommodations, which sleeps four to a room in bunkbeds built into the wall. Out back was a clothesline heavy with wetsuits; inside were a handful of guests shooting pool on a new table. Everywhere, walls were decorated with photos of standing tubes with surfers standing in them.

Françoise tapped one of the photos with her fingernail.

"Told you, Gizzy goes off," she said.

The Johns decided to head back into town for dinner, but I wanted a hot shower and a cold beer and a chance to sit on the upstairs balcony and stare at the sunset. By the time I got out of the shower, the evening sky had darkened and the temperature had dropped fifteen degrees. I changed my mind and poured myself a cup of coffee and walked out on the balcony, where an English couple sat smoking cigarettes and drinking bright concoctions.

The man hoisted his drink and told me it was composed of everything red in the refrigerator.

"Treacherous," said the woman. "Have one."

I joined them for a red concoction, and Françoise joined us for a round of who are you and where are you from. Because I was too tired to be bothered, when they asked me what I was doing in New Zealand, I told them the truth. "My mum had Lyme," said the woman, when I was done. "Got into her joints real bad. Her pinkies go three different directions now." I told her about the orthopedic surgeon who had wanted to operate on one of my knees and both my shoulders and both my elbows despite my wondering aloud if he found it odd that five major joints in my body had decided to all fail simultaneously, and for no apparent reason. "Not my department," he said. "You'll have to ask in immunology."

Françoise told us she was originally from Dunedin but now lived in Auckland, where she worked as an art teacher and actress, taking small movie roles and frequent commercials whenever she wasn't riding waves. She was often riding waves. Over the years, she'd been New Zealand's top female rider, sponsored and acclaimed, with a stroppy attitude and a reputation for big surf. Despite having retired from full-time competition, she was still ranked in the top ten.

I asked if she had ever heard anything like the Conductor's story.

"It sounds like a Maori story," she said afterward.

"Not a surf story?"

"Not many Maori who surf."

Which might not have been the case—but she spoke with authority, and was besotted with their culture. She told me stories about the Maori and how they were deliberate and crafty and intent on preserving their old ways and reclaiming their old land. "They don't just want the beach back," said Françoise, "they want the ocean too."

She was an attractive woman, full lips, long hair, a body built for tabloid scandal. We sat close on the couch and talked late into the night. Unfortunately, I had to weigh my desire for company against my desire to use my legs during the next week. My choices were sex or surf, 'cause I didn't have the strength to do both. I was on a quest, I chose surf. It wasn't the most rational of decisions, but it wasn't the most rational of years.

31

The morning brought a new swell to the beach, but the wind had not quit. The waves were big and black and cold and foreboding. Surf-starved surfers caravanned the coast, boards stacked on cars in tight bundles, checking every possible spot, for miles, in all directions. We drove along with them, but it was not to be. I was supposed to fly out of Gisborne in a few hours, heading to the South Island, while the Johns were eager to drive the other direction, chasing the swell north, chasing the promise. Françoise drove me to the airport, winked as I got out of the car.

"You should stay," she said. "The wind's gonna die; the surf will be great." She was right, but there were bills to pay, so I walked into the terminal before I could change my mind. A reporter's salary being a reporter's salary, I had financed a portion of this trip by selling a couple of articles. The main one was a preview of New Zealand's ski resorts. Unfortunately, while the South Island has the country's most famous mountains, the winter snows were still months away, so a good portion of my preview would be composed of conversations with publicists—a fact I was none too proud of.

I was thinking about this fact as I walked into the airport. The terminal was a large room, covered on one side by large glass windows looking out onto the runway and the hills beyond. Against the other side were pay phones in good working order and bathrooms that smelled of disinfectant. Between them was a small cafeteria serving coffee and cheap pastry and sandwiches thick with mayonnaise. At a small table in the middle four heavyset Polynesian women sat, chuckling and eating while a young girl played at their feet. What was so funny was hard to discern. They seemed to be speaking two or three languages simultaneously, with English occasionally peppered in. Every few minutes one of the women would reach down and cover the girl's ears, saying something, laughing hard, uncovering her ears. It must have been a routine occurrence; the girl gave the whole business little thought.

I ordered coffee and a sandwich and sat down at one of the tables to eat. In Rotorua, a few days earlier, I had met a river guide, big and thick and covered with tattoos. His name was Grant but preferred to call himself the three-hundred-pound coconut. It was his way of telling folks he was Maori in case they hadn't noticed the tribal ink covering his body. The river he liked best was called the Kaituna, a word that means "food fish," which is a fancy way of saying eels. Beside the eels, the river had three waterfalls and raging currents and bad odds. Before leading trips, Grant and his coworkers would park their boats on the banks and lead everyone in a native chant. The river was also a tribal burial ground. "We have to say a prayer before we go," Grant said, "asking permission from the ancestors to be on the river." I asked him how they knew that permission had been granted. "If you live, you know."

I was still alive, but I wasn't so sure what I knew. My entire trip seemed to have been based on whimsy. I had come to New Zealand sure that the Conductor's story would be as common as salt. I had come sure that I was a good enough surfer to hold my own. On both counts, I was wrong. Grant believed the only way to get the god's attention was through risk. "Got to be blood on the line" was how he put it.

By putting it this way, I had come to understand Grant was actually blending a number of separate lines of mythological thinking, the first being an inadvertent nod toward New Zealand's island culture, which, like most island cultures, operates with a precariously thin line between the world of the living and the world of the dead. Keri Hulme, a Maori and the 1985 Booker Prize–winning author of *The Bone People,* took her title from the traditional word *Iwi,* whose dual connotation translates to both "bone" and "tribal." When the Maori say they are "going back to the bones," they are returning to the place where their ancestors have been buried as much as they are returning to the source of their power. Grant's desire to appease the ancestors was based less on a desire to preserve the old ways than a desire to preserve his own ass.

It is difficult for a mainlander to understand the hold the dead have on the living in island cultures. Timothy White encountered a similar problem while writing *Catch a Fire,* his biography of the Jamaican reggae star Bob Marley, eventually explaining that ghost stories routinely made their way onto the front pages of the *Jamaica Gleaner,* that island's 175-year-old newspaper, which began publishing two decades before the *New York Times* and maintains a respected tradition for accuracy in reporting. While the amount of truth one wants to ascribe to such tales seems a matter of personal preference, in Jamaica, as in New Zealand, those personal preferences tend toward the supernatural. That said, a recent Gallup poll found that 69 percent of Americans believe in angels, and news of that poll became a *Time* magazine cover story.

Grant's second notion, that of utilizing risk as a way of getting closer to the gods, has a history that stretches nearly as far back as religion itself. Sweat lodges, vision quests, lenghty fasts, dangerous hallucinogens, mountain wanderings, the walkabout of the aborigines all have ancient roots. Tibetan Buddhists have long headed high up into the Himalayas with little more than sandals and thin robes to protect them from the elements. The Sioux Indians of the Great Plains practice the sun dance by slicing holes in the flesh of their breast and back. Through those holes are inserted pencil-length wooden skewers that are further tethered with strips of rawhide to a large wooden pole. The dancer must keep dancing until he has ripped the skewers completely free from his own flesh—a vision-inducing torture that can last for hours, occasionally days. These are just a few examples; the list is almost endless. Many of these activities date back to prehistoric times, and all are specifically designed to use pain and fear as triggers for mystical experience.

I got my own taste the first time I went skydiving. I was seventeen years old and terrified. The whole *let's go jump out of an airplane* concept had been dreamed up at a Friday night party, but I was soon Saturday-morning sober and somehow still going skydiving. Making matters worse, the year was 1984. While tandem skydiving had been invented in 1977, the concept had yet to make its way to the backwoods airfield in middle Ohio where we wound up. So my first jump wasn't done with an instructor tethered to my back handling any difficulties we might encounter on the way down. I jumped alone, two thousand feet and falling, my only safety net an unwieldy, old-school army parachute, dubbed a *round*. Thankfully, nobody expected me to pull my own ripcord. A short rope called a *static line* had been fixed between my ripcord and the floor of the airplane. Hypothetically, when I reached the end of that rope, it would tug open the chute. It was just that getting to this point was slightly more complicated.

At a hundred miles per hour, I had to clamber out a side door, ignore the vertiginous view, step onto a metal rung the size of a small dinner plate, vise-grip the plane's wing, lift one leg behind me and extend my arms until my body formed a giant *T*. From this awkward position, when my instructor gave the order, I had to jump. If things weren't bad enough already, the moment I leaped out of the plane—somehow—I also leaped out of my body.

It happened the second I let go. My body was already falling through space, but my *consciousness* was hovering about twenty feet away, just taking in the view. During training our instructor had explained that rounds opened, closed, then opened again in those first milliseconds of deployment. He mentioned that this happened too fast for the human eye to see, so we shouldn't really worry about it. But I was a little worried. Not only was I floating outside of my body; I was also watching the chute's open-close-open routine despite knowing that what I was watching was technically impossible to see.

While this was all going on, my body was starting to tip over, tilting into an upside-down sprawl that looked certain to produce backbreak when that chute finally caught. In what might best be described as a moment of extracorporeal clarity, I told myself to relax rather than risk whiplash. In the next instant, my chute caught. The jerk snapped my consciousness back into my body and everything back to normal or as normal as could be under some pretty unusual circumstances. While this might be neither here nor there, I never did get whiplash.

At the time, and even for years afterward, I didn't know enough about what had happened to me that day to classify the experience as a mystical anything. During those brief seconds of extracorporeality there were no visions, no feeling of divinity, no passing of secret information, no real wonderment beyond the event itself. It was just one of those things. I had almost forgotten the whole affair, but Grant had said blood for blood was the only way to get the gods' attention, and I sat down at a table in the airport to eat a sandwich and that skydiving memory came flooding back. I didn't quite know what all this meant; I just had a feeling it meant something.

32

Queenstown, New Zealand: the sun was shining and the air was crisp and the scenery looked like *The Sound of Music.* The hitch-hiker I had picked up on the way into town told me, in a manner that suggested items on a grocery list, in which of the finer local establishments it was possible to find the best of the following phenotypes: soul travelers, hippie chicks, unshaven Euros, Swedes, tomboys and dumb Aussies who love to fuck. He tossed a dime bag of marijuana on the seat on his way out of the car, saying, "Harvest time, bro, share the wealth." It was a city in gleeful disregard for the world's subtlest rules: the precarious fragility of the human body, gravity, velocity and other hard mathematical facts that bind us with ropes of consequence to our lives. In the opening pages of *Young Men and Fire,* Norman Maclean wrote, "They were still so young they hadn't learned to count the odds and to sense they might owe the universe a tragedy." He was writing about early Montana smokejumpers, but he could have just as easily been speaking of the citizens of Queenstown.

My first memory of the city belongs to a patrician Irish-woman, maybe five feet tall, whom I found sitting properly in a deck chair on the front porch of the Dairy Guest House, drinking scotch from a fine crystal tumbler. Just behind her, in the front hallway, framed certificates noted the Dairy Guest House as a finalist in the New Zealand Tourism Awards—both in 2001 and

2002—for being a boutique property unique in "hospitality, style and character," and, as such, renowned for its old-country charm and clapboard schoolhouse good looks. That these certificates announced a fame utterly incongruous with the goings-on just beyond the hotel's front door seemed a fact unimportant to all involved.

In Queenstown, you can do a different activity every day for sixty-two days in a row without repeating yourself, and since most of those activities are things like skiing, snowboarding, white-water rafting, heli-skiing, jet boating, skydiving, white-water boogie-boarding, hang gliding and other such pastimes, the city's sobriquet of "the adventure capital of the world" seems a little more than window dressing. It was here, on November 12, 1988, operating under a thirty-day permit from the New Zealand Department of Conservation, that a man named A. J. Hackett opened the world's first commercial bungee jump operation on the Kawarau Bridge, high above the gray-green torrent of the Shotover River, very close to the spot in Peter Jackson's *Lord of the Rings* where Liv Tyler conjured a flood to rescue Frodo from the Ringwraiths. In the sixteen years that have passed since that first jump, over half a million people have hurled themselves off the Kawarau's edge, so many that the Kawarau Bridge is now considered the birthplace of New Zealand adventure tourism, an industry which annually accounts for a significant percentage of the country's economy and much of its soul.

That soul was on display when I strolled out of the Dairy Guest House and onto the front porch to drink a cup of coffee and watch the sun set. The Irishwoman was sitting with legs crossed primly at the ankles, with her gray hair pushed high off her forehead. By way of introduction she asked me a question. That the question was both perfectly logical for Queenstown and perfectly reasonable for someone's patrician grandmother to be asking in Queenstown seemed a critically important notion in a way I had yet to completely comprehend. She spoke in a full Irish brogue. "Have you had a bungee jump yet?" was what she wanted to know.

I had come to Queenstown to write up a couple more ski resorts, but didn't feel like getting into it, so instead told her that I had just gotten into town and had sadly not yet had time to jump off a bridge. She told me that she was sixty-four years old and that all of those years were spent in Ireland and that today was her birthday and how do you think she spent her very first birthday away from home?

"You jumped off a bridge?"

"Did not jump a bridge," she said. "I jumped the Nevis."

The Nevis Highwire is the world's tallest bungee jump, some 440 feet and falling. Making the jump requires boarding a flying-saucer contraption called a "Jump Pod," which is suspended from a thin metal cable stretched a thousand feet across the breadth of a canyon. The view is nothing at all in every direction and, since the pod's bottom is a metal grate, a long way down. Since jumping takes place in order of descending weight, with her diminutive stature, the Irishwoman waited her turn in some sort of dizzy limbo, until everyone else had tossed themselves off the side, a process that took over an hour. Considering all there is to consider, that must have been a mighty long hour.

I had not had a bungee jump yet, nor did I have any intention of having one. When I had first moved to California, in my early twenties, bungee jumping was a nascent activity, illegal and still underground. But my curiosity was piqued by a small advertisement at the back of a local paper that offered a taste of the "bungee experience." When I dialed the number included in the ad, the phone was answered by a guy named Jeff—"no last names, not over the phone"—who claimed to be running groups out to remote bridges, often in the dead of night. There was nothing particularly sane about his operation. His equipment was homemade; his safety precautions included not giving last names over the phone and "Dude, I inspect the ropes myself." But I had no money, and he was willing to talk trade.

Because Jeff was jumping people illegally off bridges, he needed police spotters with walkie-talkies positioned five miles down the road from each end. He had done careful calculations. Five miles provided enough time to get the group off the bridge and hiding in the nearby woods. If you happened to be the unlucky jumper bobbing at the end of the rope, well, you would have to bob a little while longer.

My responsibilities included being both spotter and guinea pig. As a spotter, I was the guy who sat in the woods and watched for the cops. As a guinea pig, I was the first guy to go over the bridge's edge, the one who proved to the paying customers that they weren't going to die doing this. When Jeff told me these things, he also mentioned that he only risked a jump when he had twelve paying customers and that, since he was never exactly certain when that would happen, I would have to stay by the phone and be ready.

It was two weeks before Jeff called back. He was all business this time, giving me directions and telling me not to be late. Not being late was a consideration because he had called long past midnight and the bridge was a good five hours away. It was an all-night drive and just past dawn when I arrived. There were already a handful of people gathered on the bridge, Jeff among them. He had wavy brown hair, a small nose, a tie-dyed T-shirt. As soon as I parked my car, he told me I was ten minutes late and we had to "hurry, hurry, hurry," because the bridge was already "hot, hot, hot."

I didn't have time to ask why he was speaking in triplicate. It took less than two minutes for him to strap me into a waist harness. There was no diving board or fancy platform. I climbed over the guardrail and looked down. No reassuring water, no soft landing.

We were two hundred feet above a dry gravel bed. He told me he was going to count down from five and that I should jump on one.

"Five," he said.

It was then that I realized how little I knew about my employer. He looked like a failed engineering student who now played in a Grateful Dead cover band and spent days off taking his Hacky Sack very seriously.

"Four."

I looked down. It was a long way down.

"Three, two, one."

Saying I jumped would be an exaggeration. Saying I managed to wobble my way off the edge of that platform would be closer to the truth. The worst feeling I had ever felt I felt during those first few seconds of free fall. For a long time, I would jolt awake in the middle of the night, sweating, panting, always endlessly falling off that bridge. In jumping, I had done something that my brain couldn't process. Research done by MIT's Matthew Wilson, among others, shows that dreams are the brain's way of filing short-term memories into long-term storage compartments. Normally, because our brains don't want us to store fear, we have an emotional eraser that separates the feeling of an experience from the memory of that experience. That way, we remember that needles are sharp, but we don't remember the pain felt the first time we got pinpricked. It's our way of not recoiling in terror every time we see a syringe. But the jump had short-circuited the system. I was jolting awake at night because I couldn't file the experience in my long-term memory, because my long-term memory didn't want any part of it.

A few years after that, at a fairground on the outskirts of Toronto, I saw a bungee platform attached to the upper end of an enormous construction crane—in my memory three hundred feet tall, but, of course, that has to be wrong. It was the first time since that early morning plunge that I had seen anyone bungee jumping. I remember walking into the fairground, seeing the crane and immediately beginning to shake.

In the years since, when someone asked me what I was afraid of, my answer was always bungee jumping. Never mind that in those years, I'd accumulated a long list of other idiotic experiences; none haunted me like that bungee. For whatever reason, nothing came close. Long before I ever got to New Zealand, I had made up my mind about A. J. Hackett and all his friends—I wasn't jumping off anything.

"You should do the ledge," the Irishwoman said, pointing toward the mountain behind the hotel.

I followed her finger and saw a cable car running up the side of a two-thousand-foot cliff. At the top of the cliff, a small platform teetered over a two-thousand-foot drop. She explained that the Nevis might be the highest, but the ledge is the hardest. "They built it to be the most psychologically difficult bungee jump in the world."

"Did you jump the ledge?"

"I'm sixty-four years old," she said. "Now why would I want to something like that?"

33

That night I wandered down past the bars and the restaurants and the stores selling sweaters made from local wool and past the casino and the entrance to Eichardt's Private Hotel, which has been called "the best small hotel in the world" and "the most romantic hotel in the world," and where there are only five rooms, and each of those rooms comes with uninterrupted views and a fireplace and a mink comforter and a cost representative of such amenities. I walked by the hotel and kept going until I stood at the end of a long dock and felt the evening breeze whip off the water, and thought about the fact that somewhere very near here was the place where centuries earlier the Maori had hunted the very last flightless Moa out of existence. In that moment I wanted nothing as badly as I wanted to know if there was a word in any language for the sound of the last breath the last member of a species breathed before dying. I felt certain there had to be, but when nothing came to mind I decided it was time to start drinking.

I started drinking at a place called Bardeaux, where I learned that the gorgeous barmaid with the black hair and the glasses sadly no longer worked there. I left and walked over to the Red Rock Bar and Café, where I met a man who told me about how he cheated on his wife with prostitutes "but not with real women." I've heard similar confessions in almost every city I've visited. In one of Douglas Adams's later books, possibly *Dirk Gently's Holistic*

Detective Agency, there is a character who spends the entire book caught in the rain. Everywhere he goes rain starts falling, and everywhere he goes he hates the rain that much more. He keeps hating rain until the moment he discovers that he is a rain god. This is exactly how I have come to feel about men confessing their transgressions to me in strange bars in strange countries, and I don't think there's a word for that either.

I left the Red Rock and moved on to the Boardwalk, where I met Kujata, a man whose name comes from Islamic cosmology, referring to a gargantuan mystical bull endowed with four thousand ears, eyes, nostrils, mouths and feet. Kujata introduced me to his wife, whose name was Sarina, which is close to the American Sarah and comes from the Hebrew word for "princess." They asked me what I was doing in New Zealand, and I told them I had come with one goal—track a legend to its point of origin—but had gotten nowhere. I had talked to forty or fifty people and learned little. A quest was supposed to subsume other pursuits, not become one part of a common aggregation. I told them that I had begun to think of the Conductor as just another problem I was having, no different than job insecurities or a fight with a girlfriend.

My frustration was compounded by the fact that it'd been a few days since I'd been surfing. A couple of months back, I'd called Dr. Michael Davis at Emory University, a neuroscientist who specializes in fear, to ask him about the notion of the adrenaline junky. "Fear is an incredibly strong emotion," Davis told me. "If something scares us, the body immediately release endorphins, dopamine and norepinephrine. Endorphins mitigate pain; dopamine and norepinephrine are performance enhancers. There haven't yet been direct studies of so-called action sports, but the general scientific thinking is that the more fearful a certain sport makes you, the greater the release of these chemicals. The greater the release of these chemicals, the greater the addictionlike symptoms."

Maybe it was surf-withdrawal that was frustrating me. Maybe it was something else. After wondering why there was all this myth and magic in the Conductor's tale, I'd come to the conclusion that surfing was the bridge between such worlds, but perhaps I wasn't looking deep enough. Perhaps it wasn't surfing that was at the root; perhaps it was the neurochemical reaction triggered by all high-risk adventure. It seemed possible that the reason I hadn't figured this out was because I had yet to really scare myself.

Maybe what I really needed was a bungee jump.

34

On the island of Pentecost, in the Vanuatu archipelago, the locals practice the ritual of Naghol. Practicing the ritual involves a period of sexual abstinence, a period of fasting and a period of kava drinking—all preparations used to strengthen the participant's connection to both this world and the next. The reason one might want to strengthen such a connection is that the Naghol ritual also involves building sky-high treetop platforms, standing atop those platforms, tying a couple of vines around your ankles and leaping off. Historically, this whole scenario was something of a harvest rite, the general idea being the farther you fall, the higher the crops grow. The main crops on the island of Pentecost are yams, taro and kava. The first two are tubers, and the last is the root of a pepper plant. Curiously, all three grow underground, which makes one wonder why they were jumping at all.

In the 1970s, members of the Oxford University Dangerous Sports Club—for those unfamiliar, they really mean it—replaced the vines with rubber bands and made a series of high-profile land dives of their own. Fifteen years later, those Oxford flights inspired a couple of Kiwis—Chris Sigglekow and A. J. Hackett—and before long, folks were bungee jumping in Queenstown, perhaps inspired by the "fear of falling comes from inexperience" tagline Hackett now uses to advertise his dizzy product.

About this tagline, Hackett is only partially correct. Fear spans the spectrum of physical experience and the spectrum of emotional experience. The word originated from the Old English *faer,* meaning "sudden danger," and referred to justified fright from real menace. When fear becomes unjustified, when it produces an intense irrational state, it becomes a phobia. The word *phobia* comes from the Greek *phobos,* meaning "flight and panic and terror" from the deity of that name. According to the psychologist Donald Goodwin, a phobia is "a constant, extreme, unreasonable fear of a particular object, activity, or circumstance that leads to avoidance of the fearful situation." Without our ability to feel such fears and to pass along this information to others, humans would have vanished from this planet a long time ago. So strong is this ability that evolution has hardwired certain useful fears into our brain. Reptiles and insects and loud noises are common examples; fear of falling is another. Our fear of falling is not, as Hackett supposes, inexperience. It's basic genetics.

A small almond-shaped sliver of the brain called the amygdala generates fear. It resides in the anterior portion of the temporal lobe, deep within the limbic system. The limbic system produces our emotions, with the amygdala specializing in fear and rage. When the amygdala detects a threat, it sends out signals which trigger reflexive responses of the run-don't-walk variety. Almost immediately, the adrenal glands flood the body with adrenaline and cortisol, preparing us for swift adventure by converting glycogen into energy-rich glucose. Hearts beat faster, pupils widen, throats parch, breathing speeds up and the blood vessels close to the skin begin to contract so more blood is available for our muscles to use.

The hippocampus, the part of the brain responsible for storing and retrieving memories, is also part of the limbic system. This is because it helps to know what you were scared of yesterday in assessing threats today. If I had no experience whatsoever with falling, a cliff might make me feel fear, but it wouldn't make my palms sweat, my heart pound and my insides quiver when standing on flat land and thinking about the fact that I was planning to bungee jump off the edge of a two-thousand-foot cliff. It was not, I should mention, fear of dying that was my main concern. I had a decent understanding of the technology and safety standards and knew that the chances of a fatal mishap were exceptionally small. People who are worried about dying are worried about their landing; I was just worried about the fall.

Not only was I getting set to jump what was psychologically designed to be the most frightening bungee jump ever, but I had also decided to do so at night, because the women at the A. J. Hackett counter had told me that jumping at night makes the most psychologically difficult bungee jump in the world even more psychologically difficult. I guess I wanted it this way because what I really wanted was the jump to produce some real magic. What exactly qualified as real magic was hard to say.

The movie *Confessions of a Dangerous Mind* opens with Chuck Barris's character, played by Sam Rockwell, saying: "When you're young, your potential is infinite. You might be Einstein. You might be DiMaggio. Then you get to an age when what you might be gives way to what you have been. You weren't Einstein. You weren't anything. That's a bad moment." It had been a long time since I'd seen that movie, but when I ran out off that ledge and leaped into darkness, the only thing I remember was hearing Rockwell's voice in my head. "That's a bad moment" was what he said.

As it turned out, I did not have a transformative moment jumping the ledge. Nor did I have one jumping off the Harbor City Bridge in Auckland, which I did a few days later. I did have a conversation with a number of folks who worked for A. J. Hackett, who all told me people had profoundly spiritual experiences bungee jumping all the time. When I asked what qualifies as a profoundly spiritual experience, one of the operators said, "For most people bungee jumping is the hardest thing they've ever done. When you're done doing the hardest thing you've ever done, you feel like you can do absolutely anything afterward—if that's not a spiritual experience, I don't know what is."

The day after I jumped the Harbor City Bridge was my last in New Zealand. There was rumor of some swell in the water, so I teamed up with a surfer I'd met in Auckland and drove to the northern coast to check out Piha. When we got there, the waves were double-overhead walls, as hostile looking as any I had ever seen. My friend told me that sometime last year Pearl Jam's lead singer, Eddie Vedder, was surfing Piha on a day like this when he got caught in a riptide and had to be rescued. He thought via helicopter but wasn't certain. Vedder's reputed to be a pretty good surfer, but my friend glanced at the break and shook his head against it. "Got to be something wrong with you, surfing out there on a day like this."

We drove across the island to a beach called Te Arai. The break has something of a reputation for friendliness, but we caught it in a seriously bad mood. While the waves weren't quite snapping closed and weren't quite double overhead, they were starting to push in those general directions. Normally I'd give serious thought to paddling out at a strange break on a day this big, but I'd just jumped off the ledge and just didn't seem to mind. The paddle out took forever. I counted twenty-nine duck dives before I decided to stop counting. Much of the time I was gasping for air, my arms straining, lactic acid burning my muscles, but it didn't seem to matter. I felt like I was in a trance, beyond fear, beyond exhausting. I had one goal: I was going to get out there and catch a wave.

In the end I caught more than one. We surfed all morning and on through the afternoon. When I finally got out of the water, I was so tired it was hard to carry my board up the beach. My shoulders ached for weeks afterward; I could have cared less. I'd flown halfway around the world to fail to find the Conductor, but got to splash about without a trace of fear instead. I'd ridden the waves I'd come to ride. The playwright Edward Albee wrote in *The Zoo Story,* "Sometimes a person has to go a very long distance out of their way to come back a short distance correctly." I knew exactly what he meant.

PART FIVE

You have a lot going on, all of it weird.

—William Gibson

35

Sometime in the midnineties I ended up at a party in San Francisco with my friend Michael and his friend David and a couple of off-duty undercover narcotics agents. How the off-duty undercover narcotics agents ended up with us at this party is a long story, and not nearly as interesting as one would suspect. What is possibly more interesting is that we were all very, very stoned. We were probably too stoned to do much besides lean against a wall in the stairway of someone's two-story Victorian and stare at the steady stream of partygoers that had been trekking past, though one of the advantages of being too stoned to move is that you can get plenty of exercise simply leaning against a wall, staring at strangers.

We were leaning against the wall when somebody wondered where the dance floor was, and somebody thought outside, and somebody else thought upstairs, and some unseen obstruction caused the line to come to a sudden halt, leaving a very beautiful woman stopped directly in front of Michael. She never looked at him, never even saw him, but it was a hot night and she was wearing a tank top and her bare shoulder was a few inches from his face. Tattooed on that shoulder, in simple bold type, were three words. I put it to you that the impact of these words was perhaps augmented by what was clearly some very high-quality Humboldt County marijuana, but that does not change the fact that those three words read: MICHAEL WAKE UP!

In a very short moment an incredibly long time passed, then the line started moving again and the woman disappeared. Before anyone could say anything, Michael pushed off the wall and dashed away and caught the woman at the edge of the dance floor, which was upstairs after all. "I'm Michael," he said. "What if I'm just fine? What if I don't want to wake up?"

She didn't say anything for a minute, and then she said he didn't understand. She said she had a friend named Michael who had gone into a coma, the result of a bad motorcycle accident. The doctors were not hopeful. The family was not hopeful. Twelve friends got together and got MICHAEL WAKE UP! tattooed on their shoulders. "And then," she said, "he did."

Carl Jung came to believe that traditional notions of causality were incapable of explaining some of the more improbable forms of coincidence. In places where no clear linkage could be demonstrated between two events, but where a meaningful relationship still existed, he suspected a different principle was likely at work. Jung called this principle *synchronicity*. At his most succinct he defined his term as "meaningful coincidence" or "acausal parallelism," the slightly more intricate "an acausal connecting principle" or the excessively intricate "the simultaneous occurrence of a certain psychic state with one or more external events which appear as meaningful parallels to the momentary subjective state"—whatever the hell that means. But mostly he felt his was a principle best defined by example.

If I was trying to give an example of synchronicity, I could bring up the Michael Wake Up story. I might just as easily mention that the first time I heard the Conductor's story was in Indonesia, where it was told by an Australian with whom I had only the most casual of acquaintance; and that the second time I heard the tale I was in Mexico, where it was told by an American with whom I had only the most casual of acquaintance. It would be important to point out that I had ended up surfing with both of these men through roundabout happenstance. It would be just as important to note that on both occasions I had made a bad decision and taken a bad fall and gotten a bad beating. Afterward, in both cases, I paddled over to a small dinghy anchored outside the break to recover, and, in both cases, something in the whole deal had inspired my acquaintances to paddle over to tell me the Conductor's tale. If I was a stickler for such things, I might point out that the dinghy was anchored some distance away and that paddling over required a conscious act of will, or I might contact a mathematician who could work out the statistical probability of such overall improbability, but none of that would be necessary. Even without the help of the numbers I am a little dubious about the synchronic significance, albeit not for the obvious reasons.

What of these obvious reasons? In *The Skeptic's Dictionary,* Robert Todd Carroll writes, "Jung maintained that these metaphysical notions are scientifically grounded, but are not empirically testable in any meaningful way. In short, they are not scientific at all, but pseudoscientific." Which may not entirely be the case. Synchronicity was initially conceived while Jung was having dinner with Albert Einstein, who was then remaking a world—our own actually—into one where time and space were relative and the notion of meaningful coincidence did not violate these new rules.

Jung later developed the full theory alongside another co-conspirator, in this case Wolfgang Pauli, a professor of theoretical physics at Princeton, one of the founding fathers of quantum mechanics, and the winner of the 1945 Nobel Prize for what has since been called the Pauli Principle, also known as the Exclusion Principle, which states that no two electrons can occupy the same quantum state. Pauli is perhaps more famous for his sharp-tongued dismissal of shoddy science; once, after attending a lecture by Albert Einstein, he stood up and said, "You know, what Mr. Einstein said is not so stupid." He was also fond of saying of bad physics that it was so far off the mark it was "not even wrong," though Pauli never thought of synchronicity as bad science; he merely thought of those opposed to it as bad scientists.

In fact, Pauli is most famous for uncovering a second phenomenon which he considered an example of synchronicity, a so-called macropsychokinetic phenomenon known universally as the Pauli Effect: the mysterious failure of technical equipment in the presence of certain people. Pauli himself was cursed with the Pauli Effect. The physicist had only to enter certain rooms, and test tubes would shatter, power would cut out, vacuum seals would begin to leak. While this may seem like something of a myth, so frequent were these occurrences that the physicist Otto Stern, Pauli's good friend and fellow Nobel laureate, forever barred him from entering his lab.

Along similar lines, Pauli was keenly interested in *the fine-structure constant,* which characterized the strength of electromagnetic interaction and was denoted by the fraction 1/137. Harald Atmanspacher, in his essay "The Hidden Side of Wolfgang Pauli," points out, "The number 137 haunted Pauli all his life, and he did not get weary of stressing that its theoretical understanding would be crucial, but missing so far." It was cancer that killed Wolfgang Pauli; though he never did come to understand the fine-structure constant, he did die in a hospital in Zurich, in Room 137.

One of the most difficult aspects of quantum physics, much like synchronicity, has to do with the question of believability. The problem lies in the fact that the world of quantum physics is not the world of Newtonian physics. In Newton's world, cause precedes effect, action does not happen at a distance and things cannot be in two places at the same time, but in the quantum world, all

these things are as common as California sunshine. Three hundred
years of Newtonian-inspired rational materialism has made us believe that we live in Newton's world, though—as physicists now
agree—that is not actually the case. Right now, many believe the
world is flat and synchronicity an impossible notion. But at the
quantum level, the world is round, and synchronicity works just
fine. When it comes to reality, the truth of our Newtonian world-
view may be so far off the mark that it's not even wrong.

I present these facts to you as neither an argument for nor
against the authenticity of Jung's principle. I am merely stating the
facts of the case. At the time I heard the Conductor's tale, I did not
know these facts. I had not yet learned that the online encyclopedia Wikipedia's timeline for quantum physics does not begin, as
one would suspect, with Max Planck's 1900 black-body radiation
law—the so-called quantum hypothesis which represents the first
coherent thought anyone had on this matter—but instead with
Buddha's 585 BC supposition that "there are indivisible particles of
mind and matter which vibrate three trillion times in the blink
of an eye." I had not learned plenty. But I did know that at the core
of synchronicity was some kind of sixth-sense certitude in cosmic
connection.

Jung was clear: synchronicity does not reveal itself in hindsight. It's always an in-the-moment sensation. This is the point
that drives the skeptics mad: synchronicity can't be measured in a
laboratory. It's subjective; it's a feeling. And in those moments I
heard the Conductor's tale, I felt nothing. The only sixth-sense
certainty I had was the certainty that I was hearing a common
surfer's myth. It wasn't until I got to New Zealand that I started to
realize there was nothing common about the story and even less
common about the fact that I had heard it twice in ten years, never
mind the circumstances.

The reason I am certain that I felt nothing was that about two months after I had jumped off a ledge in Queenstown in the hope of finding true magic, on an otherwise pleasant summer evening, I felt something. I had been to the movies and was walking home, standing at the corner of Sunset and Vine waiting on a light that would not change. What I felt was a tap on my shoulder.

I turned around to find a mildly dapper older man standing a few inches away. He was maybe fifty, maybe European, with clean clothes, good boots, a mustache. I had never seen him before, and I would like to tell you that he'd never seen me before, but then he placed a small plastic lighter in the palm of my hand, holding on until he was sure of my grip.

"You need them now," he said.

"Who?"

"Yes, now, more than me."

The light changed. He dropped my arm and walked away. He had the walk of a mildly dapper older man. I watched him walk his walk across the street and down the block before glancing down at my hand. The lighter was adorned with a black-and-white photograph of Larry, Curly and Moe—the Three Stooges—whom, I guess, I needed now.

I put the lighter in my pocket and crossed the street and noticed a woman walking toward me. She was very tall and very well dressed, wearing a long gown and expensive pearls. She could have been plucked from the pages of *Vogue*. She could have been plucked from the pages of *Vogue* give or take the bright pink fuzzy bunny slippers she was wearing on her feet.

A half block beyond the woman in the bunny slippers I passed a man dressed in a Spiderman costume, yelling into a pay phone. "I can't take it," he shouted. "This job. I just can't take it." Two blocks later I came across a life-size cardboard cutout of Chewbacca. He was about eight feet high and a quarter inch wide and standing at the crosswalk. I stood next to him for a little while, trying to figure out who had put him there, when I found myself looking into a shop that sold garb favored by strippers and others who feel the need for thigh-high boots made from silk and aluminum siding. Inside the store was an old Chinese man riding a bicycle through the packed aisles, running his hands over an assortment of furry bras, crotchless panties, PVC corsets and fishnet body stockings. Was this synchronicity, or was my brain just creating patterns out of a series of random, wacky events?

Pattern recognition is the term cognitive neuroscientists use for the brain's ability to lump like with like, thus making sense of all of our experiences. It is a capacity that, as the NYU professor of neurology Elkhonon Goldberg points out in his book on the subject, *The Wisdom Paradox,* "is fundamental to our mental world . . . Without this ability, every object and every problem would be a totally de novo encounter and we would be unable to bring any of our prior experience to bear on how we deal with these objects or problems. The work by Nobel laureate Herbert Simon and others has shown that pattern recognition is among the most powerful, perhaps the foremost mechanism of successful problem solving."

So fundamental is the need for pattern recognition that it's tied to the body's reward system. When we recognize patterns, our brain releases a chemical that make us feel a little better, which may account for things like the tiny rush of pleasure that comes with filling in a crossword puzzle answer. The reason we pay attention to moments of synchronicity is that the brain has also pumped a few other chemicals into us that alert us to the fact that it's time to pay attention. The physicist Heinz Pagels writes in *The Cosmic Code* that "human beings are pattern recognizing animals *par excellence.* We can perceive distributions where other animals know only individual events . . . Is there meaning in random events? Is there a pattern?

Synchronicity refers to the psychological phenomena of attributing a pattern, perhaps at an unconscious level, to different random events."

In 1958, K. Conrad coined the term *apophenia* for the "spontaneous perception of connections and meaningfulness in unrelated phenomena." It was a rationalist's reaction to Jung's synchronicity. In Conrad's mind, apophenia was what happened when our pattern recognition skills went haywire, for example, the spiritual flipout and the conspiracy mania that often accompanies schizophrenia. Currently, the term surfaces most frequently in the debate about whether or not the sensitivity to unusual experiences is a symptom of serious mental disorder. Conrad used the term to refer to psychosis, though other researchers have since begun to suspect that apophenia is more of a bridge between creativity and psychosis, the revolving door between art and insanity.

In 2002, the Swiss neurologist Peter Brugger decided to see if people with a proclivity toward believing in the paranormal—toward a belief in such things as spirits and synchronicity and that surfing could create real magic—had better pattern recognition skills than skeptics. To test this idea, Brugger took twenty true believers and twenty nonbelievers and showed everyone a series of slides. All of the slides were of people's faces. Some of the pictures had been expertly scrambled—a nose from person A; an ear from person B; a cheek from person C—while other were actual, unadjusted, real faces. Across the board the true believers were much more likely to mistake a scrambled face for a real one than the skeptics.

Brugger then gave all of his participants L-dopa, a drug used in the treatment as Parkinson's disease, which increases the levels of the neurotransmitter dopamine in the brain. Dopamine is the reward portion of the brain's need/reward system. It's a chemical that produces the sensation of pleasure that accompanies the accomplishment of a goal. One of the reasons people find cocaine so

addictive is that it causes the brain to flood itself with dopamine—
the very drug evolution created to get us to do the things that we
need to do to survive. The slide show was then repeated with a
fresh set of faces. Under the influence of dopamine both groups
were much more likely to call scrambled faces real, but the skeptics
significantly more so. This means that those of us with more
dopamine running around our brains are more likely to notice patterns where others see none and, by extension, those of us who notice such patterns will most likely try to ascribe some semblance of
meaning to them, even if that semblance of meaning is more than
a little detached from what we think of as the rational world.

Brugger was starting to suspect he had found one of the neurochemical mechanisms for a spiritual belief, but one experiment
does not make a theory. His notion got a further boost when Dean
Hamer and other researchers began looking for a gene that encoded
for the same spiritual traits. (Their search is thoroughly and won-
derfully delineated in Hamer's aforementioned *The God Gene*.) The
end result was the discovery of VMAT2, a gene that regulates the
flow of serotonin, adrenaline, norepinephrine and, perhaps most
important, dopamine in the brain. They found that those of us
with the specific variation of the VMAT2 gene that ups the brain's
production of these chemicals are also the people who score highest on the psychological tests for spirituality. In other words, those
of us with this VMAT2 variation have greater spiritual leanings
than those without, and one of those spiritual leanings includes the
dopamine-modulated predilection for synchronicity.

If I was trying to give an example of synchronicity, I might
also mention that the movie I had come from seeing was Sofia Cop-
pola's *Lost in Translation*. I might add that I left the theater with one
particular line of dialogue stuck in my head. The line was "your life,
as you know it, is gone." It was stuck in my head when I was handed
the lighter, and it popped back in there a moment after I had

noticed the fuzzy bunny slippers. It was there during Spiderman and Chewbacca and the skipper-store incidents. I mention it as proof of nothing, or everything, or maybe something in between, but in the weeks and months to come there was one thing that was certain. My life, as I knew it, was gone.

36

That night marked the beginning of a blizzard of coincidence. There were a few at first and then by the dozen. I would get the notion in my head to call Joe, and the phone would ring and it would be Joe. And then Michael, Micah, Adam, Andrea, Shannon, Sheerly, Terena, Tess, Howard, Kevin, Chad, Jori and everyone else and over and over. I got very good at thinking of a song and turning on the radio to find it playing; I got better at thinking of someone and running into that person an hour later. These coincidences were the first of a long string of down-the-rabbit-hole experiences too numerous to recount. The novelist Michael Ondaatje once wrote, "The important thing is to be able to live in a place or a situation where you must use your sixth sense all the time," and I agree completely, but it was starting to feel like I drank the wrong Kool-Aid.

It is not easy to describe the extent of this change. It was a hundred little things; it was nothing big. I realized my feelings quite literally felt different. At first it seemed like I had opened a door somewhere inside myself, that I had access to deeper levels of emotion, but then I realized that it was the emotions themselves that had changed. It was like someone had swapped out my limbic system and given me a brand-new one. All of this might sound like a good thing if you go in for that New Age gadgetry, but really, the rave scene never did it for me and after all those years of feeling my feelings one way, having them feel radically different was a little like waking up with a new nose.

Then there were the times these new emotions did things I didn't think emotions could do. I'd be in conversation with someone else, often a stranger, and be completely overtaken by a kind of full-body empathy. I was suddenly feeling not only all of my feelings but also those of the person I was talking to as well—an experience as startling as any I can recall. James Austin, a professor emeritus of neurology at the University of Colorado, writes that such expansive empathy is a normal product of spiritual experience. In his exhaustive inquiry into the neuroscience of Buddhism, *Zen and the Brain,* Austin notes: "Zen meditation has been used to nurture empathy in psychological counselors at the master's degree level. After only four weeks of regular zazen, these student counselors increased their effective sensitivity and openness to experience." But I was not meditating; I was just surfing.

A few weeks later I was surfing a Santa Monica beachbreak. The sun was bright, the sky clear. The waves were in the head-high range, the tide heading low. I had been out for almost two hours, no great rides, a few good ones. I decided to catch one last wave and call it quits. My choice wasn't anything special, a fast right, with maybe just enough shoulder to carry me. I took a few strokes to line up with the peak, a few more to catch the wave, and then everything got quiet, too quiet. Surfing is usually accompanied by a dull roar, the constant thump of a few thousand pounds of water collapsing in on itself, but in those moments I heard nothing. The sound had just cut out. Gone elsewhere, perhaps Tahiti.

The silence caught me unawares. I looked around, trying to figure out what was happening, and suddenly realized that it wasn't just that the sound had disappeared; it was that my whole world was now moving past in freeze-frame. Time had slowed, somehow, like someone had turned the temporal tap down low. My brain and body, my thoughts and reflexes, seemed wildly accelerated, but everything else had been reduced to a lollygagging crawl. Time was moving so slowly that I could see every inch of the water, every surface nub, every shadowy nuance. It was then that I noticed my peripheral vision was extended, almost panoramic. I had the strange sensation of thinking that I was seeing out of the back of my head. And then the wave, still in slow motion, began to close out.

I watched the wall set up, the water suck off the bottom, the curl begin to pitch. There was nowhere to go, and I was certain to fall. But I didn't fall. Somehow I sucked my knees toward my chest and floated across the closeout, dropping off the far end and into the next section of wave. I made that section and then strung together a complicated series of maneuvers despite the fact that I had never done any of them before, nor had I any idea how to do them. All of this was just happening. It was clearly impossible. Mine might be a world where I knew who was on the other end of the phone before I answered it or what song was playing on the radio before the radio had been turned on—these, at least, were the kinds of anomalous events familiar to many—but a world where time slowed, where sound vanished, where vision worked in 360 degrees and I could really surf—this was an entirely new species of juju.

Unfortunately, this was not a species of juju that was meant to last. The next time I got back in the water, I had returned to my plebeian ways. Time went back to its traditional second-by-second progression. My vision was no longer panoramic, my aerial assault no longer a part of my skill set. In fact, it seemed that my entire newfound arsenal—the slashes and floaters and whatever—had been lost in the dustbin of memory. Everything had returned to normal, but suddenly normal wasn't good enough.

PART SIX

If I were called in
To construct a religion
I should make use of water.

—Philip Larkin

37

Rabbi Nachum Shifren, the author of *Surfing Rabbi: A Kabbalistic Quest for Soul,* is a tall man with a long beard and a longboard who once told me, "I don't take anyone seriously who doesn't surf," before telling me his wife doesn't surf. At the tail end of the summer of 2000, I spent an afternoon with the Surfing Rabbi riding the machine-perfect waves at Malibu. It was on that day that I saw him catch a wave and walk right up to the front of the board and arch his back and let that long beard brave the wind as he dangled ten toes over the nose, an act which he believes a form of prayer, though he also believes his whole life is a form of prayer. When he rides at Malibu, he leaves his yarmulke and Torah in a cloth bag under the second lifeguard station, right behind the volleyball court. He's got to have the Torah with him. Sometimes he surfs all day and on into the night, and then he has to paddle in to say his evening prayers on the beach. He reads his parashah right beside the volleyball court, where the beach curves slightly, where he can see both the ocean and the land. He does so with fifty other surfers watching him from the water, famous surfers and beginners, anyone at all. He doesn't care. He says that anyone who wants to can come here and surf, says the ocean's free, says that it's God's gift to the world, says that surfers understand prayer—whatever the form.

For this reason the Surfing Rabbi doesn't proselytize in the water, doesn't deliver sermons. He doesn't worry too much about surfers. He says that if you want to know God, learn to surf. He says that if you want to know God, come to Malibu. In 2005, *Surfer* magazine included an interview with the Surfing Rabbi in an article titled "Is God a Goofyfoot? If So, Surfing May Be the Next World Religion." This article begins: "We could continue to fill editorial pages for two years solely with letters written by surfers to tell us of their spiritual quests in the waves. It's a phenomenon, really. And it's one; I believe that is unique to surfing. I mean, do you think tennis players feel like they're getting spiritual fulfillment out of their daily matches? Does the mail department at *Gun World* have a hard time handling the letters from readers about the spirituality of firing a .357?"

There have been many theories about the spiritual nature of this sport, and most involve some form of watery communion. At the far end of this spectrum are the surfers who believe that since the ocean was the place where life began on this planet, the act of riding on a wave allows the surfer to momentarily connect with this living memory. In Jungian terms, surfing gives the surfer access to the collective unconscious of the planet. Perhaps it was for this reason that Timothy Leary called surfing our highest evolutionary activity.

"I was really puzzled by that Leary quote the first time I heard it," Jim White once said. "At the time, I was a professional surfer, I knew all these other professional surfers—they didn't strike me as very heavily evolved. But every time we'd go surfing, there'd be a moment when we weren't a bunch of pros in the water worrying about our standings, or what version of wiggle-wiggle-shimmy-shake we were going to try on our next wave. Every now and again all that would just disappear. We would disappear. We have all this Cartesian baggage. Life is our struggle between the desire for separation and our desire for union. But to ride a wave you have to completely forget yourself; you have to be absorbed in the moment, or you'll fall off. So every wave is about union, it's a momentary connection with something far beyond yourself, and that doesn't happen very often. Surfing may be the easiest way to access this union; surfing is like a heroin injection of union."

That notion of union has been with the sport since the days of its earliest pioneers. The entry for Tom Blake in Matt Warshaw's *Encyclopedia of Surfing* begins: "While Tom Blake can't be placed ahead of Duke Kahanamoku as the world's most influential surfer, his contributions to the sport—in terms of board design, wave-riding technique, competition, surf photography, and literature— are in many ways more tangible. 'Blake altered everything,' surf journalist Drew Kampion wrote in 2001. 'He almost single-handedly transformed surfing from a primitive Polynesian curiosity into a 20th century lifestyle.'" In 1969, in *Surfing* magazine, Blake published an early draft of "The Voice of the Atom," his wave-riding-inspired religious philosophy, the core equation of which— Nature = God—the author later carved into a rock in Wisconsin.

In the "Is God a Goofyfoot?" article, *Surfer* mentions that "the Blake mode of inquiry persisted, even if the man himself went reclusive, and in the late-'60s and early-'70s, curious surfers began to espouse various Eastern philosophies, steeping themselves in yoga and meditative practices." One of those surfers was a man named Wayne "Rabbit" Bartholomew, who won eight world tour con-tests including the 1978 world championship, thought himself a descendant of ancient mystics in the style of J. R. Tolkien, referred to Pipeline as Mordor and wrote in his autobiography: "I am the legacy of ancient warriors and kings. I've passed through the dark caverns of fear, I've overcome the pain barrier and now fully ac-knowledge my ability to fly through cliffs and shoulder the moun-tains themselves."

In the 1977 film *Free Ride*, Rabbit caught one of the longest, deepest tubes on record. He caught that tube at Uluwatu, in In-donesia, and it was because of his tube that I first went to Bali, and it was in Bali where I first heard the Conductor's tale. I once asked Rabbit if he had ever heard anything like the Conductor's tale. He hadn't, but did point out: "That does not mean to say he doesn't exist. I just don't know of the story. Back in the seventies, the few surfers who could read a weather map had a definite edge; they would magically appear on the perfect days at every classic point-break along the coast, then disappear into the shadows. I felt I was in the zone for a while. Kirra, my home break, is a bit mythologi-cal in that it is a rare catch. When construction of a boat harbor was planned, I organized a surfing competition to block it. Every year, for four years in a row, conditions were absolutely perfect, six to eight feet. It was wild; the day before [the contest] was flat every year; I would sit on top of Kirra hill the days, and nights, leading up to the weekend, and Kirra delivered. Two years in a row I was at a press conference fielding questions as to how I was going to per-form a miracle [the surf was flat] when a call came through from the bureau of meteorology that a cyclone had just formed. It was like Kirra was saving itself from destruction, appearing in all its majesty for the world to see, then disappearing."

It is also worth noting that Rabbit managed the same wave-conjuring feat for the six years he ran a similar contest at Jeffrey's Bay in South Africa, and that the day after each of these J-Bay con-tests the surf would go flat, and that in the five years since Rabbit stopped running the Kirra contest, there has never been surf for the event. "I often wonder if today's event directors prepare with the same intensity that I used to. I believe in willpower. It is quite fea-sible that there was a Conductor, a mythical wave magnet. I experi-enced it for a few seasons, and it was a deeply satisfying experience. But I maintain that Kirra was saving itself; I was just the conduit."

Rabbit is not alone in feeling like a conduit. In July of 2003, an Associated Press writer named Matt Sedensky began an article about an amateur Christian surf contest: "As the white-tipped wave melts into the ocean and the rush of adrenaline gives way to feelings of rebirth, some well-tanned surfers are making a startling discovery: They are finding God." In a recent interview Izzy and Coco Tihlanyi, the twin sisters who founded the Surf Diva Surf School, the original all-girls surf school, were quoted as calling surfing "spirituality on a stick." The author Thomas Mitchell writes in his essay "The Seven Levels of Surfers" about the Soul Surfer: "This is the highest level, the pinnacle of surfing spirituality equivalent to Nirvana, Satori, Total Enlightenment, etc. and is rarely attained. The Soul Surfer expresses himself through his unity with the breaking wave. He borrows the wave's spirit for a short while and uses his body and equipment to translate the essence of the wave's spirit into Art."

And these examples go on and on. It was apparent to me that many people thought surfing was a spiritual activity, and—if Rabbit Bartholomew's experience was anything to go by—a good number of them had encountered things far stranger than time stopping and panoramic vision along the way. It seemed to me that the answer to the question why was there all this mysticism in the Conductor's tale had everything to do with the fact that essentially the tale was nothing beyond a good surf story. But what I could do with this information was an entirely different question.

38

I didn't know what had happened to me that day surfing in Santa Monica, but I quickly found out that calling up neuroscientists to ask about the intersection of science and spirituality and surfing didn't produce the best of results. Yet I already had firsthand knowledge that skydiving could produce an out-of-body experience, and I knew that this experience was similar to some of what I felt that day surfing in Santa Monica. I figured these seemingly extracorporeal events might be a decent place to start looking for some answers.

Out-of-body experiences belong to a subset of not-so-garden-variety phenomena broadly called the *paranormal,* though the dictionary defines the word as "beyond the range of normal experience or scientific explanation." As it turns out, out-of-body experiences are neither. Despite serious skeptical misgiving, similar events have been reported in almost every country in the world. For centuries, mystics of all faiths, including the world's five major religions, have told tales of astral projection. The entire Eckankar religion is based on the concept. Nor is this phenomenon reserved only for the religious. The annals of action sports are packed with it as well—from surfers hovering above the waves; to mountain climbers enjoying a bird's-eye view; to motorcyclists gliding above their bikes, watching themselves ride; to pilots floating outside their airplanes, struggling to get back inside. In her essay "The Voice,"

Grace Butcher, who held the American track-and-field record for the 880 from 1958 to 1961, described her first major race: "The starter gave us instructions, and the gun went off. I ran a few steps into a dimension I didn't know existed. Suddenly I seemed to be up in the rafters of the arena, looking down at my race far below. I could see the black framework of the high catwalks vaguely around me, the cables, the great spotlights, the blazing brilliance of the tiny track so far beneath me, and myself running in the midst of the others in my race that was clearly going on both with me and without me."

Most out-of-body experiences, however, take place not within the confines of such extreme environments but as part of normal workaday lives. While different surveys have yielded different results, even a conservative estimate shows that one out of twenty people have a story they can't quite explain, and those numbers go up substantially when you include the natural extension of the phenomenon: the near-death experience. While the incidence of the near-death experience is slightly smaller than that of the out-of-body experience—a 1990 Gallup poll found 30 million Americans have had some sort of a near-death experience in their lifetime—if you combine percentages, even the most conservative conclusion finds 10 percent of the planet's populace has shared in this type of adventure.

If you wanted to investigate this type of adventure, a good place to start would be with Dr. Melvin Morse. In 1982, while working as a brain cancer researcher and finishing up his residency in pediatrics at Seattle Children's Hospital, Morse made extra cash moonlighting for a helicopter-assisted EMT service. One afternoon, he got a call to fly out to Pocatello, Idaho, to perform CPR on eight-year-old Crystal Merzlock, who had spent a little too long at the bottom of a community swimming pool. When he arrived on the scene, she had been without a heartbeat for nineteen minutes, her pupils already fixed and dilated, but Morse was good at his job. He got her heart restarted, climbed into the chopper and headed home.

Three days later, Crystal regained consciousness. Ten days after that, Morse was back at the hospital where she had been taken for treatment. Two weeks had passed by the time they bumped into each other in the hallway. Crystal pointed at him and turned to her mother, who was standing beside her at the time, and said, "Hey, that's the guy who put the tube in my nose at the swimming pool." Morse didn't know what to do. "I had never heard of out-of-body experiences or near-death experiences. I stood there thinking: How was this possible? When I put that tube in her nose, she was brain dead. How could she even have this memory?"

Morse decided to make a case study of Crystal's experience, which he published in the AMA's *American Journal of Diseases of Children*. For categorization purposes, he labeled the event a *fascinoma,* which is both medical slang for an abnormal pathology and a decent summary of the state of our knowledge at the time. But Morse was still curious. He didn't mind that his was the first published description of a near-death experience in a child; to him it seemed like an interesting first step into a longer project.

He started by reviewing the literature, discovering that while out-of-body experiences are defined by a perceptual shift in consciousness, near-death experiences start with this shift and head on down that famous dark tunnel. On the way to the light, people report love, peace, warmth, welcome, the reassurance of dead friends, dead relatives and the full gamut of religious figures. Occasionally, there's a whole life review, followed by a decision of the should-I-stay-or-should-I-go variety. He discovered that the near-death experience's classic explanation as delusion had been recently upgraded to a hallucination produced by a number of different factors, including fear, drugs and a shortage of oxygen to the brain called hypoxia. But it was drugs that caught his eye. Morse knew that ketamine, used as an anesthetic during the Vietnam War, frequently produced out-of-body experiences. Other drugs were also suspected triggers. Morse decided to study halothane, another commonly used anesthetic, believing his study might help explain the high incidence of reports of near-death experiences trickling out of emergency rooms. "It's funny to think of it now," Morse told me, "but really I set out to do a long-term, large-scale, debunking study."

Morse's 1994 research, commonly referred to as the Seattle Study, spanned a decade. He interviewed 160 children who died and were later revived while in intensive care at Seattle Children's Hospital. All of these children had been without pulse or breath for at least thirty seconds, some for as long as forty-five minutes. The average was ten to fifteen minutes. For a control group, he used hundreds of other children also in intensive care, also on the brink of death, but whose pulse and breathing had not been interrupted for more than thirty seconds. That was the only difference. In every other category—age, sex, drugs administered, diseases suffered and setting—the groups were the same. Setting included not only the intensive care unit itself but also intimidating procedures such as the introduction of a breathing tube and mechanical ventilation. These are important additions since fear has long been considered a trigger for near-death experiences and, as Morse later explained, might have been responsible for my out-of-body adventure.

Morse graded his subject's experience according to a sixteen-point questionnaire designed by Bruce Greyson, a professor of psychiatry at the University of Virginia, that remains the benchmark for determining whether or not an anomalous experience should be considered a near-death experience. Using the Greyson Scale, Morse found that out of 26 children who died, 23 reported a classic near-death experience, while none of the other 131 children in his control group reported anything of the kind. He later video-taped these children recalling their experiences and making crayon drawings of what they saw once outside their bodies. Many of these pictures included the standard fare: long tunnels, giant rain-bows, dead relatives, deities of all sorts. But some also included pictures of the exact medical procedures performed, including elaborate details about doctors and nurses whose only contact with that child took place while that child was dead.

Other scientists have since duplicated Morse's findings. Most recently, Pim van Lommel, a researcher at Rijnstate Hospital in Arnhem, the Netherlands, conducted an eight-year study involving 344 cardiac arrest patients who died and were later resuscitated. Out of that total, 282 had no memories, while 62 reported a classic near-death experience. Just as in Morse's study, van Lommel examined the patient's records for any factors traditionally used to explain near-death experiences—such as setting, drugs or illness—and found no evidence of their influence. He too found death the only possible causal factor. He too found people with difficult-to-explain memories of events that happened while they were dead.

Possible clues to the biological basis of these unusual states turned up in studies conducted in the late seventies, when the U.S. Navy and Air Force introduced a new generation of high-performance fighter planes that generated tremendous g-forces, which, in turn, pulled too much blood out of pilot's brains, causing these pilots to black out midflight. The problem, known as G-LOC, for gravity-induced loss of consciousness, was serious, and James Whinnery, a specialist in aerospace medicine, was the man charged with solving it.

Over a sixteen-year period, working with a massive centrifuge at Brooks Air Force Base, in San Antonio, Texas, Whinnery spun over five hundred fighter pilots into G-LOC. He wanted to figure out at what point tunnel vision occurred, how long it took pilots to lose consciousness under acceleration, how long they remained un-conscious after that acceleration ceased and how long they could be unconscious before brain damage started. Along the way, he dis-covered some interesting things. He found, for instance, that G-LOC could be induced in 5.67 seconds, that the average blackout lasted 12 to 24 seconds and that forty of those pilots reported some sort of out-of-body experience while unconscious. Not knowing anything about out-of-body experiences, Whinnery called these episodes *dreamlets,* kept detailed records of their contents and began perusing all the available literature on anomalous unconscious ex-periences. "I was reading about sudden-death episodes in cardiol-ogy," recounts Whinnery, "and it led me right into near-death experiences. I realized that a smaller percentage of my pilot's dream-lets, about ten to fifteen percent, were much closer in content to a classic near-death experience."

And then Whinnery went back over his data and realized there was a correlation: the longer the pilots were knocked out, the closer they were to brain death. And the closer they were to brain death, the more likely it was that an out-of-body experience would turn into a near-death experience. This was the first hard evidence for what had been long suspected: that the two states are not two divergent experiences, but two points on a continuum.

He also found that if G-LOC was gradually induced, it pro-duced tunnel vision. "The progression went first to gray-out [loss of peripheral vision] and then to blackout," says Whinnery. "This makes a lot of sense. We know that the occipital lobe [the portion of the brain that controls vision] is a well-protected structure. Per-haps it continued to function when signals from the eyes were fail-ing due to compromised blood flow." He also learned that upon waking up, his pilots reported a feeling of peace and serenity. In other words, Whinnery found that the pilot's transition from gray-out to blackout resembles floating peacefully down a dark tunnel, an experience much like the defining events of a classic near-death experience.

The simplest conclusion to draw from these studies is that, give or take some inexplicable memories, these phenomena are simply a collection of normal physical processes that occur during unusual circumstances. After all, once scientists set aside the traditional diagnosis of delusion as the source of these states and began looking for biological correlates, there were plenty of possibilities: compression of the optic nerve could produce tunnel vision; neurochemicals like serotonin, endorphins and enkephalins could help explain the euphoria; psychotropics like mushrooms and mescaline often produce vibrant hallucinations from the past. However, no one has directly tested this hypothesis.

What researchers have studied are the effects of the near-death experience. Van Lommel conducted lengthy interviews and administered a battery of standard psychological tests to his study group of cardiac arrest patients. The subset that had had near-death experiences reported more self-awareness, more social awareness and deeper religious feelings than the others. Van Lommel then repeated this process after a two-year interval and found the group that had had near-death experiences still had complete memories of the event, while the others' recollections were strikingly less vivid. He also found that the near-death group had an increased belief in an afterlife and a decreased fear of death, while those without the experience showed the exact opposite. After eight years, he again repeated the whole process and found those two-year effects significantly more pronounced. The near-death-experience group was much more empathetic, emotionally vulnerable and often showed evidence of increased intuitive awareness—while still exhibiting no fear of death and a strong belief in an afterlife.

Morse too did follow-up studies long after his original research. He also did a separate study involving elderly people who had a near-death experience in early childhood but were now well into old age. "The results were the same for both groups," said Morse. "All of the people who had had a near-death experience— no matter if it was ten years ago or fifty—were still absolutely convinced their lives had meaning and that there was a universal, unifying thread of love which provided that meaning. Matched against a control group, they scored much higher on life-attitude tests, significantly lower on fear-of-death tests, gave more money to charity and took fewer medications. There's no other way to look at the data. These people were just transformed by the experience."

Morse's work caught the attention of Willoughby Britton, a clinical psychology doctoral candidate at the University of Arizona who was interested in post-traumatic stress disorder. Britton knew that most people who get up-close and personal with death tend to have some form of post-traumatic stress disorder, while people who got that close and had a near-death experience have none. In other words, people who have a near-death experience have an atypical response to life-threatening trauma—and no one knew why.

Britton also knew about work done by the legendary neurosurgeon and epilepsy expert Wilder Penfield in the fifties. Penfield, one of the giants of modern neuroscience, discovered that stimulating the brain's right temporal lobe—located just above the ear— with a mild electric current produced out-of-body experiences, heavenly music, vivid hallucinations and the kind of panoramic memories associated with the life-review part of the near-death experience. This helped explain why right temporal lobe epilepsy was a condition long defined by its most prominent symptom: excessive religiosity. And given what Whinnery has found, it is possible that his pilot's out-of-body dreamlets were related to moments when blood flow to the right temporal lobe was seriously compromised.

Britton hypothesized that people who have undergone a near-death experience might show the exact same altered brain-firing patterns as people with right temporal lobe epilepsy. The easiest way to diagnose temporal lobe epilepsy is to monitor a person's brain waves during sleep, when there is an increased likelihood of activity indicative of epilepsy. Britton recruited twenty-three people who had had a near-death experience and twenty-three who had not undergone either a near-death experience or a life-threatening traumatic event. Working at a sleep lab, she hooked up her subjects to electrodes that measured EEG activity all over the brain—including the temporal lobes—and recorded everything that happened while they slept.

She then asked a University of Arizona epilepsy specialist who knew nothing about the experiment to analyze the EEGs. Two things distinguished the group with near-death experiences from the controls: they needed far less sleep, and they went into REM sleep far later than normal people. "The point at which someone goes into REM is a fantastic indicator of depressive tendencies," said Britton. "We've gotten very good at this kind of research. If you took one hundred people and did a sleep study, we can look at the data and know, by looking at the time they entered REM, who's going to become depressed in the next year and who isn't." Normal people enter REM at 90 minutes. Depressed people enter at 60 minutes or sooner. It works the same in the other direction. Happy people go into REM around 100 minutes. Britton found that most of her near-death-experiences group entered REM sleep at 110 minutes. In other words, she was the first person to find an objective neurophysiological correlate which supported the anec-dotal evidence that the near-death experience is a seriously trans-formative experience.

Britton thinks the near-death experience somehow rewires the brain, and she found evidence to support her hypothesis regarding the temporal lobe: 22 percent of her near-death group showed tem-poral lobe synchronization, the same kind of firing pattern associated with temporal lobe epilepsy. "twenty-two percent may not sound like a lot of anything," says Britton, "but it's actually incredibly abnormal, so much so that it's beyond the realm of chance." She also found something that didn't fit with her hypothesis. The temporal lobe synchronization wasn't happening on the right side of the brain, the site that had been linked in Penfield's studies to the religious feelings in epileptics. Instead she found it on the left side of the brain. And a lot of people are very uncomfortable with that fact.

The reason they're uncomfortable has to do with work done over the past ten years by a number of different scientists, including the neuroscientist James Austin from the University of Colorado, the neuroscientist Andrew Newberg and the late anthropologist and psychiatrist Eugene D'Aquili from the University of Pennsylvania, the same researcher who had studied ritual behavior in wolves. By doing SPECT (single positron emission computed tomography) scans of the brains of Buddhist monks during meditation and Franciscan nuns during prayer, these scientists pinpointed, in far more exacting detail than Penfield achieved, the exact locations in the brain that were most active and most inactive during periods of profound religious experience. They found a marked decrease in activity in the right parietal lobe, a part of the brain often called the Orientation Association Area because it helps us orientate ourselves in space. It allows us to judge angles and curves and distances, to know where the self ends and the rest of the world begins. People who suffer injuries in this area have great difficulties navigating life's simplest landscapes. Sitting down on a couch, for example, becomes a Herculean task since they are unsure where their own leg ends and the sofa begins. The SPECT scans showed that meditation temporarily blocks the processing of sensory information from the parietal lobes.

When that happens, as Newberg and D'Aquili point out in their book *Why God Won't Go Away*, "the brain would have no choice but to perceive that the self is endless and intimately inter-woven with everyone and everything the mind senses. And this perception would feel utterly and unquestionably real." They use this to explain the interconnected cosmic unity that Buddhist monks experience, but it works just as well to explain what Morse called the "universal, unifying thread of love" that people with near-death experiences consistently reported.

The brain scans show that when the parietal lobes go quiet, portions of the right temporal lobe—some of the same portions that Penfield showed produced feelings of excessive religiosity, out-of-body experiences and vivid hallucinations—become more ac-tive. They also found that certain activities often found in religious rituals—like rhythmic drumming and repetitive chanting—produce just this kind of effect. A finding that helps explain some of the more puzzling out-of-body reports, like those of the airplane pilots suddenly floating outside their planes. Those pilots were intensely focused on their instrumentation, much in the way that meditating monks are focused on mantras. Meanwhile, the sound of the engine spinning produced a repetitive, rhythmic drone much like tribal drumming. If conditions were right, said Newberg, these two fac-tors should have been enough to produce the same temporal lobe activity that triggers an out-of-body experience.

The neuroscientist Michael Persinger of Laurentian University in Sudbury, Ontario, has conducted other studies that explore the generation of altered mental states. Persinger built a helmet that produces weak, directed magnetic fields. He then applied these fields to over nine hundred volunteers, mostly college students. When he lit up the temporal lobes, Persinger's helmet produced the sort of mystical free-of-the-body experience common to right temporal lobe epileptics, meditators and people who have had near-death experiences.

None of this work is without controversy, but most scientists now agree that our brains are wired for mystical experience. This is not, as all of these researchers are quick to point out, proof for or against the existence of God. Instead, it is proof that these experiences are as real as any other, since our involvement with the rest of the universe is always mediated by our brains. Whether this is simply right temporal lobe activity, as many suspect, or, as Britton's work hints and Morse believes, a whole brain effect remains an open question, but the general feeling is that we'll have the answer sometime soon. Persinger thinks there is a simple explanation for why people with near-death experiences have memories of events that occurred while they were apparently dead. The memory-forming structures lie deep within the brain, he says, and they probably remain active for a few minutes after brain activity in the outer cortex has stopped. Still, Crystal Merzlock remembered events that occurred more than nineteen minutes after her heart stopped. Nobody has a full explanation for these phenomena, and we are left in that familiar mystical state: the one where we still don't have all the answers.

39

On a summer day in 1984, the writer Rob Schultheis was climbing alone, high in the Colorado Rockies, on a mountain called the Neva. Schultheis, as recounted in his cult classic *Bone Games: Extreme Sport, Shamanism, Zen, and the Search for Transcendence,* reached the summit around noon. Within seconds, bad weather set in. He was carrying crampons and an ice ax, both absolute necessities if he was going to make it back down, except there was now enough electricity in the air that both tools were hissing and crackling and shooting off sparks. Suddenly, he was alone on a mountaintop, in the middle of a lightning storm, the tallest metallic object within a hundred miles.

He should have gone back the way he came, but panic being panic, Schultheis sprinted across a knife-edged ridgeline in desperate search of a shortcut. The path grew thin, then thinner. On either side of him were massive cliffs. He stumbled on, terrified, as the rain turned to snow. Within minutes, the ground was too slick, the way down too hard. It took him no time at all to get good and stuck. When he tried getting unstuck, he slipped and slid and wound up hanging from a rock. He hung on until his fingers went numb. A long fall and a nasty tumble landed him on a tiny ledge. One of his knees was crushed; there were deep cuts on his legs and more on his back. The weather was getting worse. His choices were freeze to death or down-climb what was a clearly a treacherous slope for skilled rock climbers under the best of conditions. He was not a skilled rock climber. These were not the best of conditions.

Tears were running down my face; I wept like a small boy, with fear, hurt, and the shame of being injured. I wanted someone to take my hand and lead me home, but that's not the way it works. I was on my own, alone. I got to my feet, retrieved my ice axe and crampons, strung them on my back, and like a sleepwalker began to make my way down the precipice.

Something happened on the descent, something I have tried to figure out ever since, so inexplicable and powerful it was. I found myself very simply doing impossible things: dozens, scores of them, as I down-climbed Neva's lethal slopes. Shattered, in shock, I climbed with the impeccable sureness of a snow leopard, a mountain goat. I crossed disintegrating chutes of rock, holds vanishing under my hands and feet as I moved, a dance in which a single missed beat would be fatal. I used bits of rime clinging to the granite as fingerholds. They rattled away into space but I was already gone, away . . . .

Looking back on it, I really can't explain or describe properly that strange person I found inhabiting my body that afternoon. It was just too different from my everyday self, and I have never seen its like before, nor have I seen it since . . . The person I became on the Neva was the best possible version of myself, the person I *should have been* throughout my life. No regrets, no hesitation; there were no false moves left in me. I really believe I could have hit a mosquito in the eye with a pine needle at thirty paces; I couldn't miss because there was no such thing as a miss. It didn't matter whether I fell or not, because I couldn't fall, any more than two plus two can equal three.

Afterward, Schultheis wanted that feeling back, and when he could find no easy way to obtain it, decided to make a thorough study of such extreme states. He found that his few hours of transcendence, far from being a unique event, were close to common in the world of high adrenaline. In 1892, the Swiss geologist Albert von St. Gallen Heim collected dozens of similar accounts in his monograph, *Remarks on Fatal Falls*. In 2004, the editor Garth Battista collected almost fifty more tales in his *The Runner's High: Illumination and Ecstasy in Motion*. There are hundreds of other examples. Charles Lindbergh described similar experiences in his account of his solo flight across the Atlantic, and Yvon Chouinard did the same for an eight-day ascent of Yosemite's El Capitan. John Muir wrote of a time when he was trapped and terrified on a cliff face in the Sierra Nevadas: "I seemed suddenly to be possessed of a new sense. The other self, bygone experience, Instinct or Guardian Angel—call it what you will—came forward and assumed control. Then my trembling fingers became firm again, every rift and flaw [in the rock] was seen as through a microscope, and my limbs moved with a positiveness and a precision with which I seemed to have nothing at all to do. Had I been borne aloft upon wings, my deliverance could not have been more complete."

In early 2005, I got to know the rock climber Michael Reardon. Unlike most other climbers who place nuts and cams and other forms of protection into the rock as they ascend, Reardon is a soloist. For the past eighteen years he has climbed with shoes and a chalk bag and nothing else. "If I fall, I die" is how he explained it. He routinely climbs at an expert level, consistently pushing the upper limits of his sport to the edge of comprehension. In 2004, at

Temple Crag in Big Pine, California, he soloed Dark Star, the longest route in the Sierras, a three-thousand-foot thirty-four-pitch monster that usually takes two days to tackle. He did it in five hours, in the dark, with only one shoe because he lost the other a third of the way up. When he finished that climb, he soloed three similar routes before the sun went down.

So intense is his focus while soloing that Reardon likens the experience to "climbing inside an eight-foot egg-shell," beyond the confines of which his senses simply do not register. A few years ago, 110 feet off the ground on a route in Joshua Tree, a gargantuan barn owl flew out of a crack in the rock inches above him. So close was the bird that he could count its tail feathers, but he barely noticed. Later he described the experience: "It was like a very small voice in my head said, 'Oh look, that's an owl,' and then I made my next move." Reardon frequently starts such days in the dead of night, occasionally moonless ones. "It's an open-senses experience," he says. "I'm thousands of feet off the ground and can't see anything, but somehow I always know where the holds are." As novelist Thomas Pynchon once said, "Sure this is magic, but not necessarily fantasy."

The University of Missouri criminologist David Klinger made a study of police officers in gunfights in his book *Into the Kill Zone,* reporting everything from cops who never heard gun blasts despite weapons being fired inches from their ears to cops whose sense of time had slowed down enough that they saw the bullets they had fired actually strike their targets. Malcolm Gladwell explored Klinger's explorations in his book *Blink,* writing: "Our mind, faced with a life-threatening situation, drastically limits the range and amount of information that we have to deal with. Sound and memory and broader social understanding are sacrificed in favor of heightened awareness of the threat directly in front of us." He went on to describe how the basketball player Larry Bird used to say that at critical moments in the game, the court would go quiet and players would seem to be moving in slow motion.

Bird is not alone. As the psychologist Mihaly Csikszentimihalyi pointed out, flow states are common in almost every experience if conditions are right. Athletes of all sorts speak of being in the zone, and nearly everyone who's played a game understands their extraordinary benefit. In these states everything works: football players make spectacular diving catches between four defenders, basketball players sink shot after shot no matter the obscenity of the angles involved, and, occasionally, surfers like myself find themselves frozen in time, linking maneuvers they had never tried before. The range and depth of this experience vary considerably, but exceptionally heightened performance accompanied by exceptionally heightened pleasure are the most consistent markers. Michael Sachs, a Temple University sport psychologist who has also made an extensive study of flow states—defined for his purposes as "increased sense of well being, an enhanced appreciation of nature, and a transcendence of time and space"—found they vary from pleasant highs to nearly unbearable bliss. At the far end of the spectrum sits a new species of juju: a Schultheis-like sense of power and invincibility, out-of-body experiences, the occasional orgasm.

Much of what we understand about flow states first emerged in the seventies, when scientists decided that runner's high was a by-product of endogenous—meaning internal to the body—opioids called endorphins. These chemicals kill pain and produce happiness much like exogenous—meaning external to the body—opiates like morphine, opium and heroin. There are at least twenty different endogenous opioids and most are not completely understood, but we do know that the analgesic power of the principal endorphins released during times of stress can be a hundred times stronger than morphine.

But endorphins are only one small piece of a much larger puzzle. Extreme stress also causes the release of enkephalins, a neurotransmitter similar to endorphins in analgesic ability but also responsible for modulating mood-enhancing and performance-enhancing chemicals like serotonin, dopamine, norepinephrine and epinephrine. While the relationship between these chemicals and runner's high has often been presented as concrete and absolute, there are still plenty of unanswered questions. So many in fact that in May of 2002, Huda Akil, a University of Michigan endorphin researcher and then president-elect of the Society of Neuroscience, told the *New York Times* science reporter Gina Kolata that "this endorphin-in-runners is a total fantasy in the pop culture." It was a statement that, for many, became the last word on the subject. Though Kolata herself hedged a bit in her book *Ultimate Fitness,* deciding that running makes people high, some people think this may have something to do with endorphins, while others do not. Put simply: something's happening here; what it is ain't exactly clear.

Other scientists haven't been as quick to dismiss the anecdotal evidence, instead beginning to look into the purported effects of runner's high and their similarity to so-called spiritual experiences. When moving in this direction, they have zeroed in on those chemicals downstream from the enkephalins. Serotonin, for example, the chemical that jump-started our Prozac Nation, has been much touted for its mood-enhancing abilities, but lately more attention has been paid to its psychedelic past. It was the discovery of LSD that led us to the discovery of serotonin because LSD, and other psychotropic substances like psilocybin, mescaline and DMT, all bond to the same receptor sites as serotonin. Since these drugs have been anecdotally famous for their abilities to produce quasi-mystical experiences, scientists have recently begun looking into this possibility with newfound interest. In 2003, the *American Journal of*

Psychiatry reported that a team of Swedish researchers working with brain scans discovered a correlation between the presence of serotonin-regulating receptors in the brain and a person's capacity for self-transcendent experience. Add in Peter Brugger's dopamine research, and the case becomes ever stronger. In fact, all of the neurochemicals that show up during times of extreme stress are the exact same neurochemicals that the geneticist Dean Hamer linked to VMAT2,—the gene he dubbed "the God Gene."

Researchers have also found that the same endogenous opioids released during runner's high are also present during moments of important social bonding, parental love and, apparently, during *the chills*—those transcendental emotional experiences that occur while listening to music. Jaak Panksepp, head of affective neuroscience research at the Chicago Institute for Neurosurgery and Neuro-research, has spent much of the past decade studying the chills and has observed the mechanism in humans and a host of other animals. "In one widely cited study," writes Steven Johnson in his book about the neuroscience of everyday experience *Mind Wide Open,* "he [Panksepp] played dozens of records to chickens attached to equipment designed to record their shivers of pleasure. The chickens turned out to have the strongest positive response to the late-era Pink Floyd record *The Final Cut.*" This is important information since, from an evolutionary perspective, if spirituality really is biological, that biology should be found not just in human beings but in lower orders as well.

More recently, the neuroscientist Arne Dietrich reopened the runner's-high debate when he found high levels of anandamide in young men during exercise. Anandamide, from the Sanskrit word for *bliss,* is a cannabinoid, a tiny fatty acid naturally occurring in the body and known to produce sensations of pain relief and happiness similar to those of THC, the psychoactive ingredient in marijuana. (When people smoke pot, the THC binds to the anandamide receptor in the same way that heroin binds to the endorphin receptors.) Because marijuana features so prominently in a number of major religions, in the seventies scientists began looking into its relationship to the feelings we most often describe as spiritual. The Psychologist Charles Tart found that 65 percent of his extensive pot-smoking study group reported feeling more open to experience, childlike and filled with wonder than his controls. Twenty-five percent felt joyous, peaceful, in touch with the divine and connected to the universe. In other words, the chemistry that brought us the Age of Aquarius is the same chemistry that brought us runner's high.

Why humans would want to produce psychotropic states during extreme exercise is a puzzle that scientists have only recently begun to crack. The answer is far from definitive, but they have come to suspect that these flow states may be the by-product of one of the traits that separate humans from other animals: an ability to run exceptionally long distances. Humans can, in fact, run longer distances than any other species on Earth. John Skoyles and Dorian Sagan write about this in *Up from Dragons,* their fascinating study of the evolution of human intelligence.

> We are great long-distance runners; if need be we can keep up a steady fast pace from dawn to dusk. Records in older editions of the *Guinness Book of World Records* show that people can run up to 188 mi within 24 h and up to 621 mi in a single 136-h and 17-m stretch. And we can do it with heavy loads: Sedan chair bearers walked 30–35 mi each day. Many non-Westerners, both men and women, are reported to carry "light" loads of 60 lbs for 25–40 mi over rough landscapes. There is a report of one group of Chinese schoolgirls who regularly walked 50 mi daily. In the manhunt for the outlaw (and Indian runner) Willie

Boy in 1909, when horsemen came within 20 minutes of catching him, he increased his stride into 5-foot paces. He carried on like this for 15 miles, and the horses were forced to stop and rest. He managed to outrun his pursuers for 500 miles. In Mexico, Tarahumaran runners in kickball races covered 150–300 mil over 1–2 days—more than six marathons. Imagine a chimp running even a few yards and you'll see how radically our legs have turned into efficient long-distance running machines. No other primate—or any creature, for that matter—is so specialized for endurance.

For millennia, humans fed themselves by running down their prey. From every continent come stories of epic hunts that make our most grueling marathons pale by comparison. With so much of our time spent chasing our food, it makes sense that those of us who found a way to produce pain-numbing neurochemicals like endorphins would be more successful hunters than those who suffered every step. Just as those of us who developed the ability to produce performance-enhancing neurochemicals like dopamine, serotonin, epinephrine and norepinephrine—helping us run faster, jump higher, swim farther—would have an easier time than those without this edge. Better, faster, stronger means more food and less danger, which mean longer lives and more children. In other words, from an evolutionary perspective, the ability to find this strange, sometimes spiritual, zone is a trait we have cultivated since our body's chemistry first figured out how to cultivate the experience.

While this helps clarify some of the science of spirituality, it doesn't quite explain why *Surfer* magazine can fill storage rooms with letters blathering about the mystical reverence practitioners feel for their sport. After all, people talk plenty about the Church of Gridiron, but that doesn't mean *Sports Illustrated* has dedicated an issue to the possibility of football as a new religion. To the best of my knowledge, there's no skydiving imam or NASCAR high priest. As strange as it may be, there seems to be something in surfing that produces self-transcendent states more often than in other sports. What that thing is remains a matter of some debate, though a good case can be made for the neurochemistry that results from the two-step process fundamental to the sport: first you have to catch a wave; then you have to ride that wave.

Catching a wave, especially in big surf, feels a bit like falling from a skyscraper. The speed itself is enough to produce an adrenaline rush, but the size of that rush is directly proportional to our perception of danger. Since catching a wave is also the time when the ferocity of the ocean is closest, vulnerability is at its highest and the worst wipeouts consistently occur, that perception is quickly ratcheted upward. Add in the solo nature of the sport, the lack of protective gear and the sense of strangeness that comes with trading familiar dry land for the foreignness of water, and you begin to understand the potential for serious neurochemical reaction.

But it's not just danger that modulates that reaction; we also know it to be greatly enhanced by the novelty of the situation. Since the devil we don't know often scares us more than the one we know, the more we perceive the situation as unique, the greater our need for neurochemical response. By definition, because every wave is different, every wave is also novel. This feeling gets further amplified by the rarity of good waves, an even greater rarity of big waves, the five-second length of a typical ride, the seven-wave average for most surf sessions and the lack of predictability in weather patterns—all of which limit one's ability to prepare for situations. Pretty soon you soon start to understand that surfers are often operating in foreign waters, far outside of their comfort zone, which, as it happens, are also the perfect conditions for producing transcendent experiences.

And catching a wave is only the first part of the equation. Riding a wave requires an exquisite amount of pinpoint concentration and, as years of meditation research have shown, that pinpoint concentration is also a trigger for mystical states. "The intense focus surfing requires is so similar to the intense focus of deep meditation or ecstatic prayer or ritual dance or any number of so-called spiritual experiences," the neuroscientist Andrew Newberg once told me, "that it's a pretty good bet that very similar things are going on in the brain." In other words, the Orientation Association Area—the part of the brain that helps us distinguish between self and other—is going to go quiet, producing the feeling of interconnected divine unity that the Canadian psychologist Richard Burke called *cosmic consciousness*. Simultaneously, the temporal lobes—the part of the brain that Wilder Penfield and many others have found to produce intense spiritual experience—get energized.

Certainly there are many other activities that require just this kind of laserlike focus, but unlike surfing, most of those do not take place on a constantly shifting surface. Basketball has an incredible variety of moving parts, but the court doesn't change shape every time the players begin play. Action sports may offer better comparisons but still come up short. Snowboarders huck huge cliffs, but they land on solid ground. Skaters don't find the half-pipe rearranging itself midway through their ride. What's more, in surfing, either you go from that heightened adrenaline state produced by catching a wave directly into the incredible Zen-like focus needed to ride a wave, or you fall down—there's no other way to participate. While there's not yet enough research to back this up, it seems likely that surfing's one-two combo of adrenaline rush and meditative rush is enough to send things spiraling toward funkytown with a frequency not found in other sports.

PART SEVEN

You want to carry straight on until you reach the Aleph. Then take a left. After that, it's the second, maybe third, continuum on the right.

—Alan Moore

40

It was spring of 2005. The weather had turned warm, and the waves had grown small, and my health was still no picnic. I had, like many with old wounds, become an expert at selective recall. The time before illness had become something of a cantankerous in-law, to be visited only briefly, and with the utmost caution. I took little comfort in the fact that in recent times, Lyme disease had gone from being a peculiar ailment on the edge of mainstream medical radar to becoming the largest epidemic in America, outpacing even AIDS by most counts. This led to some new drugs, a vaccine; later those drugs were found ineffective, the vaccine recalled for bringing more trouble than it cured. I was still sick, still single, still able to make green beans in the Szechuan style, but had finally bought a new couch. It was more comfortable than the old couch, which may have been the kind of thing that passes for progress; mostly it was hard to tell. From this new perch the future was still the future, a rabbit hole of uncertain friendliness, to which there was no other recourse beyond the cold plunge.

It was almost a year ago that I had returned from New Zealand, and the majority of those intervening months were spent not addressing the pivotal center of my errant quest, but rather studying the somewhat more ephemeral aspects of its biology. I had read books and talked to scientists and come to some understanding of how surfing produced transcendent experiences and even gotten a taste of such experiences myself, but I had not found the source of the Conductor's myth. So one April morning I decided to try the cold plunge. I decided to fly to Hawaii, to look for the story in what was perhaps the most obvious place one could look for such a story, but a place that had long been hidden from my view.

At first, my lack of clear sight had stemmed from the tale itself. My Aussie friend had thought the surfers involved were Kiwis. This idea was bolstered by the myriad of mythologists I had spoken to who all seemed to agree that there was something vaguely Maori about the tale. Then there was the fact that none of the California surfers I had asked had heard anything about the Conductor, and since California surfers had been round-tripping it back and forth to the Hawaiian Islands for over fifty years, I made a critical error of extrapolation. But really, looking back on it, I think the real reason I didn't think about coming to Hawaii was that I had been avoiding thinking about Hawaii for almost all of my adult life.

It was partially Chris Marchetti's fault. Chris was the man who had taught me to surf. He was also a man obsessed with Hawaii's Bonzai Pipeline. Back before that motorcycle accident took his life, Chris rode a strange five-finned surfboard called a Bonzer and became so obsessed with the possibility of surfing the Bonzai Pipeline on his Bonzer surfboard that the words *Bonzer Bonzai* became alliterative code for all the great things he would accomplish in his life. Chris was buried back in his home state of Georgia, but we had a small service for him in San Francisco and a surf at Bolinas because he would have wanted it that way. I don't remember if it was at the funeral or during the surf that I promised Chris to someday brave Pipeline in his name, but I do know that for the next fifteen years I studiously avoided the topic.

Pipeline sits on the so-called seven-mile miracle of Hawaii's North Shore, a rugged stretch of Oahu coastline that runs from the small town of Haleiwa down to Sunset Beach. The early Hawaiians called the waves at Sunset Beach *Paumalu,* or "taken secretly." Then the secret got out. From September through May brutish storms in the North Pacific send waves thousands of miles unhindered until they reach forty of the most famously treacherous surf breaks on Earth. As Matt Warshaw points out in his *Encyclopedia of Surfing,* "The power of the North Shore surf, combined with shallow reefs, crowded lineups (pressuring surfers to try marginal waves), and the near-constant surf media presence (encouraging them to take star-making risks), made this the most dangerous surf area in the world." In short, I had avoided thinking about Hawaii because I was downright terrified of the place.

Once I finally got on that plane, I couldn't get my promise to Chris out of my mind. So on the morning of my first full day in Hawaii, I drove across the island and stood in front of Pipeline. Since this wave has been featured in nearly three quarters of all the surf movies ever filmed, I knew exactly what it would look like. But the thing that none of those films seems to capture and the thing that imprints itself immediately is the rough-and-tumble aspect of the whole vista. The thing that one notices is not merely the ferocity of this or that wave so much as the ferocity of all the waves, the whole place in general, much of the damn island really. And it's in that moment when one starts to understand how good a job the tourism industry has done selling their hang-loose, *shaka brah* brand of pina-colada-ism and how utterly divorced that version is from reality. I was standing on the beach in front of Pipeline for less than thirty seconds before a pair of Japanese tourists asked me to take their photo beside the sign reading: DANGEROUS SURF. Neither seemed to notice that my hands were shaking when I snapped the picture.

I watched the wave for as long as I could watch the wave and then walked back to the parking lot and called Tom Stone. At the time I called him, I knew almost nothing about Hawaii and even less about Tom Stone. I knew that he was a professor of Polynesian history and culture at the University of Hawaii and that sometime ago, I believe a couple weeks after I returned from New Zealand, someone I had spoken to suggested that if there was anybody who might know anything about the Conductor's legend it might be Tom Stone.

As it turned out, Tom had never heard of the Conductor, but he did know about *The Wind Gourd of La'amaomao,* an ancient Polynesian myth that he thought perhaps could have become the Conductor's story. He said he taught a version of the myth in his classes and would be glad to send me a copy, also mentioning that there are a few key details of the myth that take place on Hawaii's North Shore. The last thing he told me was that if I ever decided to come to town, he would be happy to give me a tour. I told him I'd call him back as soon as I'd read the book.

Tom had been good to his word. Moses K. Nakuina's *The Wind Gourd of La'amaomao* was in my mailbox three days later, but despite all the time I'd spent chasing the Conductor's myth, the book stayed closed on my nightstand. It stayed that way for months. I can't tell you why I couldn't open the book other than the fact that opening it might mean discovering that Tom Stone was right, that the myth was of Hawaiian origin. If that did turn out to be the case, I knew I'd have to go to Hawaii, where, I also knew, I'd at least have to try to keep my promise to Chris. In fact, I was so terrified of the whole concept that I didn't even bother to phone Tom Stone back for almost another year.

When I finally did call him back, I still hadn't been able to open the book. Perhaps I was hoping he would rescind his promise to show me around the North Shore, and that would be enough of an excuse for me to cancel my trip. When I finally made the call, so much time had passed between our conversations that I had to remind him who I was and what he had offered. There was a long pause on the other end of the phone, and I thought for a second that I had somehow escaped. All he said was, "Just give me a call when you're on the island."

In the end, there was nothing else to do. The next time I called Stone was from the parking lot a couple hundred yards from Pipeline.

"You're calling me from Pipeline?"

"Yeah."

"Your first time ever seeing it?"

"Yeah."

He wanted to know what I thought, and because I didn't really know why I had called Tom Stone from in front of Pipeline and because I didn't know what else to say, I told him that I wasn't just terrified of surfing Pipeline, I was terrified of surfing anywhere on the whole damn North Shore. Because I knew nothing about Hawaii and little about Stone, at the time I was calling him to tell him I was standing in front of Pipeline I had no idea that he had made his name surfing Pipeline in the sixties, being one of the first to ride this wave from behind the curl.

Since Pipeline breaks in six feet of water and since beneath those feet is a bed of jagged lava, the lip—the front edge of the breaking wave—is the most dangerous spot to be. Pipeline's lip weighs several tons and routinely maims and occasionally kills, so the surfers who ride there, at least until guys like Tom Stone came along, would pull into the tube from in front of the curl. They would accomplish this by making the drop and then slowing down—either by pushing down their back foot and stalling their board or by dragging a hand across the wave's face and letting friction do the trick—and waiting for the tube to catch up to them. Taking off behind the curl means taking off on the far side of that crushing lip and ducking through the tiny opening at the back end of the barrel in the hopes of making it out the front end intact. Stone once lost all of his upper teeth on a day he didn't quite thread that needle. Instead, he went face first into the reef. At the time I heard that story, I was sitting with a couple of Hawaiian lifeguards—routinely thought of as the toughest watermen on Earth. Afterward they made sure I understood. "Most go face first, die going face first."

Nor did I ever bother to glance at the Tom Stone entry in Warshaw's aforementioned *Encyclopedia of Surfing,* which begins: "Stylish Hawaiian goofyfooter surfer, best known for his clean, cool lines at Pipeline. Stone was born in Honolulu in 1951, and began surfing at age four in Waikiki. He twice made the cover of *Surfer* magazine in the early 1970s, was invited to the 1970 and 1971 Expression Session events, and was featured in period surf movies including *Pacific Vibrations* (1970), *Cosmic Children* (1971), and *Five Summer Stories* (1972). Stone was addicted to cocaine by 1973, and was sent to prison after a drug bust in which he held a half-dozen people at gunpoint, including two policemen." I did not know that Stone has since gotten out of jail and gotten his life back together. In hindsight, considering everything that was to happen, of all the things I didn't know about Tom Stone, perhaps the most ironic was that I didn't know he was Hawaiian.

"Respect," Stone told me that day on the phone on the beach at Pipeline, then told me to call him back in a few days so we could get together and talk La'amaomao. "Get some waves in the meantime" was what he said before he hung up. I stood in the parking lot and looked at Pipeline for a long time before I realized that he had meant it wasn't terror I felt while looking at that wave for the first time. It was respect.

41

Tomorrow it may be paradise, but for now it is night and too dark to see. There's only the distant lap of the ocean and the subtle sixth sense of endless, empty space that one feels when alone in the middle of the Pacific. I am 2,000 miles from California and 3,800 miles from Japan and 2,400 miles from the Marquesas, a day-old arrival on the world's most isolated landmass: the deep-water volcanic archipelago—137 islands by the official count—known globally as Hawaii. The word *Hawaii* itself contains three parts, starting with *Ha,* or "breath of life," moving through *Wai,* which is often rendered as "fresh water" but literally means "any fluid besides sea water"—thus coconut milk, male ejaculate and woman's menstrual fluid also qualify—and on to the final *I,* which does not easily translate but suggests the vocal tone used by the supreme creator to sing the world into existence. All together *Hawaii* means "the breath of life that comes from the water of life that comes from the ultimate creator"—a nesting-box theology that still filters through much of Polynesian thinking.

This nesting-box theology is present in Hawaii's creation saga—the two-thousand-line cosmogonic chant known as *Kumulipo*—which accurately spans the whole of evolution, beginning in primordial darkness and ending in the late seventeenth century, along the way establishing both a divine lineage from men to kings to gods to god, but also detailing all the stars and plants and rocks

223

and animals known to the islanders. The result is a genealogy so complete that scholars still marvel that nearly two hundred years before Charles Darwin proposed his origin of species, the Polynesians had come to understand that the rhythm of life always progresses from the simplest forms to the most complex. It is also for this reason that when you hear Hawaiians talk about how much native blood they have running through their veins, they are in fact really talking about how much of the old gods are contained within themselves.

In more familiar terms, the Polynesians trace their native blood back to the Old Babylonian Era, between 1500 and 1000 BC, around the time Hammurabi was ruling in Mesopotamia and Tutankhamen in Egypt, when—in the general vicinity of what is currently considered Indonesia—an aquatic warrior people had taken it upon themselves to start sailing tiny boats across three thousand miles of open ocean because somebody got it into his head that there was another island out there. They navigated solely by starlight and magic—the ancient wayfinding belief that if you visualize your destination and stay true to your course, you will arrive. When they were done, they had populated the whole of the Polynesian triangle—New Zealand to Easter Island to Hawaii—becoming, as Captain James Cook once noted, "the most extensive nation on Earth."

The most extensive nation on Earth was also a nation of wave riders. In *Surfing: A History of the Ancient Hawaiian Sport,* Ben Finney and James D. Houston write that "those early canoe voyagers—who initiated the exploration and colonization of the Pacific some four thousand years ago—developed rudimentary board-surfing: primarily a children's pastime practiced with short bodyboards. As their descendents pushed farther into the Pacific, they carried their pastime with them. Then, on some of the main islands of East Polynesia it came to be taken up more and more by adult men and women using larger boards. Finally, along the shores of the Hawaiian Islands, surfing reached its peak. There the feat of standing erect on a speeding board found its finest expression."

But all those years of wave-riding history were almost completely erased after the European arrival in Hawaii in 1778. "We went from grass shack to high-rises in a hundred years" is a comment frequently heard in the islands. It is not simply a summation of technological progress. In the centuries that followed, the native population dropped from four hundred thousand to forty thousand, decimated by new diseases to which they had no inborn immunity and by Western notions of private property to which they had no inborn immunity. The effects—as described by Ben Marcus in his essay "From Polynesia, with Love"—were felt everywhere.

> When Captain Cook arrived in Hawai'i, surfing was deeply rooted in many centuries of Hawaiian legend and culture. Place names had been bestowed because of legendary surfing incidents. The *kahuna* (experts) intoned special chants to christen new surfboards, to bring the surf up and to give courage to the men and women who challenged the big waves . . . Before contact with Cook's crew, Hawai'i was ruled by a code of *kapu* (taboos) which regulated almost everything: where to eat; how to grow food; how to predict weather; how to build a canoe; how to build a surfboard; how to predict when the surf would be good, or convince the Gods to make it good. Hawaiian society was distinctly stratified into royal and common classes, and these taboos extended into the surf zone. There were reefs and beaches where the *ali'i* (chiefs) surfed and reefs and beaches where the commoners surfed. Commoners generally rode waves on *paipo* (prone) and *alaía* (stand up) boards as long as 12 feet, while the *ali'i* rode

waves on *olo* boards that were as long as 24 feet . . . By the time Captain Cook and his ships reached the Hawaiian Islands in 1778, the art, sport and religion of surfing had reached a sophisticated peak. But what Cook and Lieutenant King described in Tahiti and Hawai'i was the zenith of the sport in Old Polynesia, because in the wake of the *Resolution* and the *Discovery,* Hawai'i and Hawaiian surfing fell into decline for more than 150 years. *Haole* and Hawaiian cultures were thrown together in swift collision at the end of the 18th century, and within the first 20 years of the 19th century, Hawai'i was changed forever. In 1819, less than 50 years after Cook made contact with the Hawaiians, Liholiho, the son and successor of Kamehameha I, publicly sat down to eat with his mother and other high chiefesses. Men eating with women had been taboo since the beginning of time, but Liholiho had been swayed and overwhelmed by the overpowering influence of *haole* culture. His defiance of a cornerstone taboo sent a message throughout Hawai'i that the old system of laws was no longer to be followed, which dealt a fatal blow to the *kapu* system. As the *kapu* system crumbled, so did surfing's ritual significance within Hawaiian culture. Now a commoner could drop in on a chiefess without fear for his life, or even giving up his *lehua* wreath. The end of the *kapu* system also brought about the demise of the Makahiki festival, the annual celebration to the god Lono in which surfing played an integral role. But now that the Hawaiians had been set adrift from the old ways, Hawaiian culture fell into chaos.

Coincidentally, less than fifty years after the Hawaiians had accidentally mistaken Captain Cook for their own god Lono, about a

year after the overthrow of the *kapu* system, a few months after the
Polynesians had finished burning their temples and wooden idols,
when they were rootless and godless for the first time in their history, the royal high priest Hewahewa had a vision. "The new God
will soon land yonder," he is supposed to have said. And within
weeks of his pronouncement the first Calvinist missionaries arrived
on Hawaiian shores.

They didn't much like what they saw there. "The appearance
of destitution, degradation, and barbarism, among the chattering
and almost naked savages, whose heads and feet, and much of their
sunburnt skin, was appalling. Some of our number, with gushing
tears, turned away from the spectacle. Others, with firmer nerve,
continued their gaze, but were ready to exclaim, 'Can these be human beings? Can such a thing be civilized?'" was how missionary
Hiram Bingham described first contact in a letter he sent home to
his native Boston. It was also Hiram Bingham who converted
Queen Kaahumanu to Christianity, but it was she, with a convert's
zeal, who banned surfing and dancing and singing and general
nakedness on principle and the native Hawaiian tongue for good
measure.

What was the crime of the Polynesians so terrible that Hiram
Bingham could not bear to watch? seems like the kind of question
one might encounter in an *Island Living* edition of Trivial Pursuit.
Cannibalism, perhaps, or maybe a war party intent on murder. In
this particular case the Hawaiians had ventured through the waves
to greet their new guests, by most accounts bearing leis and other
gifts. But they had paddled surfboards through the waves. Surfing
was the crime so terrible.

42

It was my third day on the island and a balmy eighty-four degrees. I was buying a seven-foot-four minigun at Kimo's Surf Hut. The hut was three rooms empty of everything save surfboards and Kimo, who does not believe in false advertising. "Other people have surf shops and just sell clothes," said Kimo. "I have a surf shop and sell surfboards." Sometimes Kimo's wife, Ruth, worked behind the counter. "People don't just come here to buy a surfboard," she told me. "They come here to buy a bit of Kimo." Kimo himself had little to say on the matter.

I tucked my board under my arm and walked back out into the sunshine. In the distance were mountains so verdant that the greenery looked like wax drippings. There was some discussion about how to fit the surfboard into the car, but there was no discussion about where to go. It was early May, and the waves witnessed two days ago at Pipeline were long gone. Common consensus was that they had been the last big swell that would strike that part of Oahu this season. Now it was late spring, and late spring meant south swells, and south swells meant Waikiki—which was, after all, the birthplace of modern surfing and perhaps the only appropriate place to ride my first Hawaiian surfboard on my first day surfing in Hawaii.

Waikiki—the two-mile stretch of offshore reef breaks and onshore high-rise hotels and crowded beachfronts and high-end retail therapy extending from the leeside shadows of Diamond Head to the Ala Wai Yacht Harbor—is the only place I know where one can eat a cheeseburger at Cheeseburgers in Paradise—over 1,400 people served daily—while listening to a nicely dressed Hawaiian gentleman doing more than passable Neil Diamond covers. It was here in the early portion of the last century that the Olympic Gold medal water poloist and swimmer Duke Kahanamoku alongside the Irish-Hawaiian surfer George Freeth reintroduced the sport of surfing to their native culture, and everybody else for that matter. It was Duke Kahanamoku who would often slow down in swimming races so he would not beat the competition too badly, and Duke Kahanamoku who may have been the purest embodiment of surfing's aloha spirit, and Duke Kahanamoku whose bronze statue stands over seventeen feet high on Kuhio Beach. People are still angry that the statue faces outward toward the street, rather than inward toward the ocean. But it was George Freeth who taught a visiting journalist named Jack London to surf in Waikiki. London's description of the sport and the place, appearing first in 1907 in the *Woman's Home Companion* and four years later as a chapter in his legendary travelog, *The Cruise of the Snark,* both started the false rumor that surfing was the sport of kings—a misinterpretation of London's first line: "That is what it is, a royal sport for the natural kings of the earth"—and later provided one of the most elegant descriptions of wave riding in history.

> And suddenly, out there where a big smoker lifts skyward, rising like a sea-god from out of the welter of spume and churning white, on the giddy, toppling, overhanging and downfalling, precarious crest appears the dark head of a man. Swiftly he rises through the rushing white. His black shoulders, his chest, his loins, his limbs—all is abruptly projected on one's vision. Where but the moment before

was only wide desolation and invincible roar, is now a man, erect, full-statured, not struggling frantically in that wild moment, but standing above all, calm and superb, poised on the giddy summit, his feet buried in churning foam, the salt smoke rising to his knees, and all the rest of him in the free air and flashing sunlight, and he is flying through the air, flying forward, flying fast as the surge on which he stands. He is a Mercury—a brown Mercury.

There was talk on the beach of an approaching swell, but little sign of it in the water. I paddled out for head-high Canoes, the most central of Waikiki's twenty or so breaks, alongside several hundred other surfers and an assortment of semitreacherous watercraft. There are a dozen places to rent foam surfboards on the beach at Waikiki and several hundred men and women willing to give instructions to those riding those foam surfboards, and nearly all of those people ride the inside section of Canoes. The outside section is bigger and slightly less crowded, but that's not saying much. The online wave-riding bible *Surfline* describes the best board for Canoes as a pintail or an outrigger. The *pintail* is another word for a gun and a reference to those near-perfect days when Canoes stops being a soft, slow slide and becomes a hallowed, hollow racetrack; the *outrigger,* a reference to the double-hulled canoes that carry tourists back and forth through this lineup with a certain malicious alacrity.

I paddled into the lineup, sat up and looked around. There were surfers everywhere. Directly beside me was a sumo wrestler who seemed to have some authority. He caught my eye and said, "Brah, don't waste," and then pointed at an oncoming lump some fifty yards away. Some twenty yards later, that lump hit the reef and jacked into a wave, and I would like to tell you that I remember every detail of this moment, but there really wasn't time. I spun my board and made a quick drop and a couple of arcing turns, and somewhere between the realization that I had been given my first wave in Hawaii and the realization that I was actually riding a wave in Hawaii, I carried too little speed into my cutback and let the inside section slip away. As I popped off the back, I caught sight of a sumo wrestler hanging ten off the wave behind mine.

I caught a few more rides, but the crowds sent me down the beach toward the next break over. By the time I got to Queens, a newly arriving swell had started to show, and Queens was twice as big and twice as crowded as Canoes. I sat beside a seventy-two-year-old man. I knew he was seventy-two years old because he looked at me when I arrived and said, "I'm seventy-two years old and just started surfing." There was a younger man sitting beside him. "You can't say you've started surfing until you actually catch a wave," he said. "Fine," said the older man, "I'm seventy-two years old, and I just started paddling."

I caught a mushy left and a crowded right, and the sun was starting to drop, and I was starting to get cold. There was more swell showing at the next break over—I didn't actually know what it was called—and while there seemed to be a dozen people out there, very few of them seemed to be riding waves. Before I had time to think things through, I decided to paddle over; before I had finished paddling over, I decided that maybe I should have thought things through.

Besides the North Shore, my second biggest Hawaiian surfing fear involved heading out on an otherwise manageable day and suddenly finding myself at one of the outer reefs, very tired and a long way from shore, when the wave size went from small to medium to large in the matter of minutes it took such things to happen on this island. And the closer I got to that next break over, the more certain I felt that this was exactly what was happening.

In the fifteen minutes it took to get there, I watched waves that were pushing overhead when I started—already the lower edge of my comfort zone—begin pushing toward double by the time I arrived. When I finally reached the lineup, I realized the reason so few people were taking off on waves was that the waves were growing set by set and most people had yet to figure out exactly how big this swell was going to get and exactly where the lineup was supposed to be. I also realized that the reef, which had been mostly unnoticeable at those other breaks, was directly beneath the surface at this one. Just sitting still, I could reach down in places and touch a toe to rock. When the big sets came, the water was sucking hard enough up the face that coral heads were popping up. And the big sets were starting to come.

Finally, I paddled to a spot that I was sure was far enough outside the break that even if a sneaker set came I would be safe. My plan was to sit out there and grow old. There was one other guy out with me, and not knowing what else to do, I asked him what this place was called. "This place—Publics." Then he pointed at a wave cresting on the next reef out. "That place—Outer Castles. Very special. Very special day when Castles breaks."

Outer Castles is the name of the outside reef at Waikiki. It stretches across the whole of the bay and rarely breaks, but in the early days of the sport it was thought of as surfing's finest experience. It was here in 1917 that Duke Kahanamoku caught—by his own often understated estimates—"a thirty-foot blue bird." It is important to understand that Hawaiians measure waves by the size of the back and not the front, and since the back is usually half the front, that blue bird he caught had a face roughly the size of a five-story building. At the time, he was riding a sixteen-foot board made from *williwilli* wood known as an *olo*. The literal translation of the word *olo* is "phallus"—a reference to the big balls it took to ride the Hawaiian surf. Those boards weighed around 150 pounds and were nearly impossible to turn, but on that day Duke had little intention of turning. He rode that wave for a mile. In an interview given four decades after the fact he said, "If I hadn't fallen, I would have gone right into Happy Steiner's Waikiki Tavern."

I was staring at Castles when I saw another set appear on the horizon. I realized a number of things nearly simultaneously. The sun was now completely hidden behind a cloud, and a wind was starting to whip across the bay, and the slight shivers I had been feeling for the past few minutes were slowly becoming the full-on shakes. My hands were so cold that my fingers were starting to lock into place and I was losing sensation in my toes. What part of this was fear and what part cold, I have no idea, but I was pretty certain I didn't have the strength left to paddle in. It seemed my only choice was to catch the first wave of this set because this set looked bigger than any of the previous ones, and even if I managed to paddle over its initial offering, I didn't have enough in the tank to make it over whatever was behind it. If I didn't catch this wave, I was going to end up beneath it, suddenly rather cozy with the coral heads in the impact zone.

I was out of options, so I turned and did what the whole damn lineage of surfers who had also found themselves in this situation had done throughout the whole of time that surfers had been finding themselves in this situation: I went for it. And at the moment I felt the wave start to lift my board, I had the strangest of sensations: I realized I had been here before. I had finally gotten to the point in surfing where waves with some heft were no longer complete strangers; perhaps they were not quite friends, but at least we had something of a shared history.

In technical terms I was feeling the first bit of dopamine rush that meant my brain's pattern recognition abilities were kicking into gear. In nontechnical terms I was stoked and on my feet and driving down the face and feeling the spray exploding at my heels and feeling that deep thrum of excitement so otherworldly that the inventors of this sport had developed an entire panoply of surf gods and goddesses to worship for just this experience. I rode that wave nearly to shore, and when I finally dropped to my belly to paddle the rest of the way in, I remembered the ubiquitous bumpersticker PRAY FOR SURF was not just some pithy idiom, rather the literal translation of an ancient Hawaiian prayer.

43

A few days later, Tom Stone called and invited me over for a barbecue. The directions he gave me to his house did not strike me as the kind of directions a college professor would typically give. Among other suggestions, his included: trying not to drive into the ocean, heading straight up the mountain, keeping on when the pavement ran out, taking a left at the bent coconut tree, taking a right at the VW buses. He was waiting for me beside those buses, wearing a pair of pale surf trunks and a tank top, both emblazoned with the name of one of his surf sponsors. That a fifty-four-year-old man should have a surf sponsors tells one a number of things about the abilities of this fifty-four-year-old man.

He did not look fifty-four. He might look forty-four. His hair was dark brown and close-cropped. His arms were braided with muscle, his legs more substantial than his arms. There were reef scars on his hands and knees and several larger scars dotting his back, the result of his attempt to offer a particular kind of Hawaiian assistance to a woman who was being severely beaten by her knife-wielding boyfriend. Sometime later, when I asked him if he would be comfortable with me writing about those knife scars, he shrugged and said, "Write whatever you want; just write that the other guy looked a lot worse than this when things were done."

Which is pretty much how things go in paradise. When the sunscreen finally stops dripping into your eyes and those palm fronds get pushed out of the way, it can be a different view. When Polynesians say *aloha,* they touch foreheads and noses and inhale the same air. *Aloha* translates to "sharing spirit." It means about the same thing that Rastafarians mean when they say *I and I.* "I and I, they say, meaning you and me, meaning we're all in this together," as the reggae historian Michael Thomas wrote in *Babylon on a Thin Wire.* And out here in paradise, together can just as easily mean warm embraces as cold fisticuffs, 'cause out here in paradise, that's how affection gets done.

Two days after this evening, I would attend a small barbecue at Relson Gracie's house. There are very few true celebrities in Hawaii, but Relson Gracie is an eighth-degree red blackbelt and the second eldest son of Helio Gracie. Helio Gracie is the grandmaster of Gracie Ju-jitsu and out here that counts for something. Gracie Ju-jitsu may not be exactly familiar, but the current thinking on the topic runs that in the entire history of martial arts no other fighting style has ever proven as deadly effective. In just about every no-holds-barred combat situation in the last fifty years—including both professional bouts and amateur streetfights—Gracie practitioners have routinely bested any and all comers to the point that any and all comers are now either versed in Gracie technique or unwilling to step into the ring. The barbecue was attended mostly by Relson's close friends and prized students—a rough collection of the finest fighters on an island that loves to fight—who laughed and talked and exchanged recipes for banana bread that included the dictate "succulent, brah, you want it moist," while everyone ate grilled meat with their fingers from a communal cutting board—'cause that's also what they mean by *aloha.*

At the time I walked into Tom's backyard, I had not even learned this much about Hawaiian culture. Instead I took a seat on a rattan couch and looked around at the group of people who one way or another held the keys to my future. I soon met Tom's wife, Anne, who smiled and shook my hand, and I thought things were looking up. Then I met Tom's best friend, Pake Ah Mow, a beast of a man with the general demeanor of a Komodo dragon. He grunted and then passed out on the couch. Whatever hope I had felt moments before quickly returned to deep trepidation.

Not knowing what else to do, I sat down in a corner beside a Texan named James Fulbright who was in town making a documentary called *Miles to Surf*. The film was about the addictive properties of surfing and the lengths surfers will go to get their fix. James himself lives in Galveston, Texas, where good surf is an infrequent guest. To get his fix, he discovered that the supertankers heading up the Houston Ship Canal produce a head-high wave that runs for miles. The water is less than two feet deep in places and the canal's bottom a junkyard of scrap metal, but the real concern is that a wrong move surfing supertanker waves could get you sucked into the ship's turbines. An average ride at Pipeline lasts about ten seconds. The current record for supertanker wave-riding time in the Houston Canal holds at twenty-two minutes. A few years ago, Dana Brown put tanker surfing into *Step into Liquid,* and I wrote a story about it. It took James and me around twenty minutes to figure out that two years earlier we had spent a few hours on the phone and two years later we're going to spend a few hours sitting in Tom Stone's backyard in Oahu. "It's a cosmic convergence of like-minded individuals," said James. I could only hope so.

James was at Tom Stone's because Tom has spent the past fifteen years trying to revive a number of ancient Hawaiian practices, including *papa holua*—the sport of sledding. A *holua* sled weighs over seventy pounds and runs about fifteen feet in length and is essentially a narrow wooden ladder with two long wooden skates running beneath each side. The ancient Hawaiians used to ride them down lava chutes as a way of worshiping the volcano goddess

Pele. It wasn't uncommon for the sleds to hit sixty miles per hour; nor was it uncommon for sledders to be maimed or killed in the process—which was considered part of the fun of worshiping Pele. "It's also what we did when the surf went flat," said Tom, "you know, to get our fix."

It was around this time that Pake woke up from the couch and apologized for grunting and passing out. He had torn his rotator cuff at work a couple weeks back and had surgery just this morning. When I asked why he wasn't home and heavily sedated, he lifted his beer can and said: "No worries, brah. Plenty sedated." Even plenty sedated he was six-foot-four with huge shoulders, a big belly and a sleeve of tribal tattoos. He works as a lifeguard and rescue craft operator on the east side of the island and comes from a family of watermen. His father was Clifford Ah Mow, who helped settle one of the most vituperative arguments in nautical history. For much of the last century, there's been a question as to how the first settlers actually got to Hawaii, *accidental drift* versus *purposeful voyaging* the two contending theories. At stake was whether or not the Polynesians had the skills to sail intentionally across open ocean sans map or compass. In the mid-seventies, two Hawaiians—Herb Kane and Tommy Holmes—and one haole—Ben Finney—decided to build a traditional double-hulled ocean canoe and sail by starlight across the whole of the Polynesian triangle. The canoe was called the *Hokule'a,* but Herb Kane called it the *"Spaceship of Our Ancestors."* In 1976 Clifford Ah Mow was one of the fifteen men who made the first successful trip from Hawaii to Tahiti.

As the evening went on, Tom asked me to retell the Conductor's myth. It was the first time since I started doing so that story was not met with blank stares and uncomfortable silences. "Plenty people done plenty things to learn to call the waves," says Pake. "Brah, you go surf triple-overhead. Talk about the rush, get addicted to that rush. Yeah, people done plenty things to call the waves." Pake himself has never really learned how to call the waves but does remember a day when he took three hits of acid and paddled out on a triple-overhead day at the remote outer North Shore reef Phantoms. "Redemption day. Never had one like that since. Wipe out just sit at the bottom talk to the fishes."

Later, after the food had been cleared away and all of the wine and most of the beer drunk, Tom pulled me aside and broke the bad news: "La'amaomao was a Hawaiian goddess who controlled the wind and the waves. When she died, her bones were put into a gourd, and whoever controlled the gourd and knew the proper chants could control the wind and the waves. I think your Conductor myth is what happened when some Californian came here in the sixties, got strung out on surf and acid and the whole vibe. I think he heard the story and messed up the retelling. I think that's how things went from La'amaomao to the Conductor."

"You're telling me I've spent three years chasing some hippie's fuckup?"

"That's what I'm telling you," said Tom. Then he started to laugh, and I started to laugh, and he put his arm around my shoulder and said, "Welcome to Hawaii."

44

Hunter Thompson once came to Hawaii to cover the Honolulu Marathon and ended up so strung out on surf and acid and the whole vibe that he came to believe he was possessed by the god Lono. Historians believe that Lono began as Ro'o, a cloud-floating deity from the Tahitian canon. By the time Lono drifted over to Hawaii, he had come to control storms of all kinds, including both fertility and the good Dr. Thompson. Lono wasn't the only bit of force majeure to drift over. "Wind imprisonment by noted magicians occurs in other South Sea areas," writes Martha Beckwith in her classic *Hawaiian Mythology*. In the Cook archipelago, the high priest had a calabash containing a miniature universe. There were thirty-two holes drilled into this calabash, one for each of the winds of the compass. These were the holes in the horizon through which the wind god Raka played the world like a set of panpipes. When an open-water voyage was being undertaken, the high priest would cover all the holes but the one for the wind required by the voyage's trajectory. When that trajectory finally pointed the Polynesians toward Hawaii, Raka's magic calabash had become the wind gourd of La'amaomao.

To understand how one controlled the winds with a gourd is to understand the peculiar personal nature of Hawaiian magic. The local word for spiritual power is *mana*, the life force that flows through everything. People can have great mana—and great mana can be cultivated through deeds or practice—but it's only on loan from the universe proper. "It's like the Force in *Star Wars*," Tom Stone said. When boats shipwreck in the waters near Molokai, corpses wash up on Sandy Beach in Oahu. In older times, fishermen prized fishhooks shaped from the femurs of drowned sailors. Because Hawaiians believe that a person's mana is stored in their bones—and because the power would be squandered if those bones were not properly cared for—having one's femur turned into a fishhook was one of the things that kept people awake at night.

La'amaomao's mana was stored in her bones, and her bones were stored in the wind gourd. During the early fifteenth century, in the era of kings, when Keawenuia'umi ran the show on the Big Island, the wind gourd was given to his royal wayfinder Paka'a. In *Ruling Chiefs of Hawaii* Samuel Kamakau describes Paka'a's navigational skills: "He knew how to tell when the sea would be calm, when there would be a tempest in ocean, and when there would be great pillows. He observed the stars, the rainbow colors at the edges of the stars, the way they twinkled, their red glowing, the dimming of the stars in a storm, the reddish rim of the clouds, the way which they move, the lowering of the sky, the heavy cloudiness, the gales, the blowing of the ho'olua wind, the a'e wind from below, the whirlwind, and the towering billows of the sea."

It was Paka'a's mother who gave him the gourd and taught him the names of the winds. Each was associated with a place—Ma-ua is the wind of Niu, Holouha is of Kekaha—or an attribute: "The wind of Le'ahi turns here and there." It was also his mother who told him the bones within the gourd were the bones of his grandmother and that his grandmother happened to be the wind god La'amaomao. Thus the verses found in *The Wind Gourd of La'amaomao* represent both a magician's handbook and a Hawaiian genealogy—though in Hawaiian genealogies *grandmother* can be a slippery term typifying a line of kinship far more than a two-generational link.

The actual story retold in *The Wind Gourd of La'amaomao* is one of palace intrigue. Paka'a's divine heritage is concealed from any and all at his birth. An absent father, a difficult family life; eventually he ascends to the position of wayfinder. Jealous enemies conspire against him, usurping his position as royal navigator, forcing him to flee. Later, after Paka'a summoned the requisite assassin storm, those usurpers are drowned in the waters off Molokai and his righteous place is restored. In the chant there's no mention of whether the corpses of his enemies eventually washed up on Sandy Beach, so we'll never know if their bones were carved into hooks and their flesh used for shark bait.

We do know there are two places on the North Shore that feature prominently in the tale: a set of rocks offshore of Waimea and lonely Kaena Point. "We had enough problems, as I recall, without having to come face to face with the Genuinely Weird," Hunter Thompson wrote in *The Curse of Lono*. When Tom Stone took me to visit Kaena Point, Thompson's line came back to me, slowly starting to make more than just a little sense in that particularly Hawaiian way that such things can often start to make more than just a little sense.

45

They call Kaena Point a *leaping-off place*—this spooky spit of lava rock and desolation hung off Oahu's northwest corner—for the souls of the dead must first come through Kaena Point before making the leap to the next world. Po was that next world, the land of the gods, and Kaena Point was the gateway to Po. The natives knew better than to mess with the place. It was untamable and intent on staying that way. Some sugar baron once squandered millions trying to build a plantation on the ridgetop, and when he finally gave up, the military came in and failed to build a road there. "We were in a place that was utterly lost. Its human history could have been written on a fingernail," wrote Rob Schultheis in *The Hidden West*. He was talking about the canyons of Anasazi country, but he could just as easily have been talking about the jagged coastline and barren hills of Kaena Point.

Tom and Pake drove us out there so I could see the place where Paka'a once sailed ashore and the filmmaker James Fulbright could see Oahu's last remaining *holua* slide. We drove west until the road turned to dirt, the dirt to lava, and the lava ran right into the ocean. We passed a car flipped all the way over, its roof crushed, its tires pointed straight at the sky. We were passed by a teenage marine bounding over the deep ruts in his jacked-up truck with wheels the size of small wars. "Hoo-ah," said Pake. "Gonna drive straight to Iraq, gonna drive right off the land and keep on going."

We couldn't keep on going, so we parked and walked the rest of the way. There was no sign of Paka'a and little left of the *holua* slide, but you could see enough of the track to know that this was one of those places where the sleds hit sixty miles per hour and the natives left limbs and lives behind. "It's a several-thousand-year-old skatepark on the western tip of oblivion," said Tom.

"Good fishing," said Pake.

Pake and I walked closer to the water so he could give me a lesson in the good fishing. We stood at the edge of the cliff and looked off into that vast blue distance. Pake pointed out the rocks that squid liked to hide beneath and the dark spots where the big fish swam, the rips that would hold you and the channels that might help. He wanted to come back and dive here when his shoulder healed. I didn't want anything to do with the place. The Pacific covers one quarter of our planet, and Kaena Point gets the brunt of it. *Surfer* magazine once speculated that this may be the most concentrated spot of ocean energy on Earth. Back in the sixties, Greg Knoll took a picture here, long considered the largest wave ever photographed. A leaping-off place was right. Someone had carried an old rocking chair out there and perched it atop that cliff. It sat lonely on a flat shelf of rock, facing outward, facing vast ocean.

Pake could count the hours since he last surfed, the days until the doctors would let him back in the water. There was too much time in too many directions. He couldn't look too long at the ocean, so we headed back to find the others. When we got to the truck, Tom and James were busy under the hood. The key wouldn't turn more than a millimeter; the whole gearbox was locked down. Pake had driven us in; Tom wanted to know what he did to shut off the engine.

"I just shut it off."

"Uh-huh."

"I just shut it off."

"How?"

"I turned the key."

"You did something else?"

"I turned the key to off."

"It's a brand-new truck with a full tank of gas."

"Wax in your ears, brah."

In traditional Hawaiian medicine, urine is used to chase away evil spirits. Page 30 of June Gutmanis's *Hawaiian Herbal Medicine* contains the following advice: "When a car stalls in a remote place, late at night, one of the occupants may urinate on all four sides of the car." We were quickly running out of other ideas.

"The gods are angry," said Tom. "Gonna need a sacrifice."

"Uh-huh," said Pake. "I'm walking out of here just fine, brah."

To prepare for all such possibilities, we got some beers out of the cooler and drank them while flipping through the owner's manual. I thought about how the car the surfers had been driving in the Conductor's story broke down in a spot just like this. Pake took off his sling and tried to stretch out his shoulder. Tom plucked at his tank top, glanced over at the *holua* slide and asked if I had been over to see the wind gourd yet.

"What?" I asked, not sure I had heard right.

"It was at the Bishop Museum. I think it got moved to the 'Iolani Palace."

"The wind gourd of La'amaomao?"

"Yeah."

"Is on display at the 'Iolani Palace?"

"Yeah."

"It's a real thing?"

"What you think, brah?" said Pake.

I thought I had spent the better portion of the past five years chasing an idea around the globe, but turns out no, brah, it's on display at the 'Iolani Palace.

"Welcome to Hawaii," said Tom.

There were thunderheads behind the hills, shadows encroaching. The truck still wouldn't start. We were running out of beer. I glanced up at the *holua* slide and noticed something unusual.

"Have you noticed that the area the slide runs through looks like, um, well, a vaginal earth sculpture?"

"It looks like a what?" said James.

"A clit," said Tom.

"A clit," Pake agreed.

"Of course it looks like a clit," said Tom. "*Kaena* means 'Red Hot.' We rode sleds here to worship Pele. She's a volcano goddess. This is Pele's point. Now show her some damn respect."

"I am showing her some damn respect."

"Good," said Tom.

And then Pake turned the key, and the truck started.

46

The 'Iolani Palace is the only palace ever built on American soil. Construction began on December 31, 1879, the day was Queen Kapi'olani's birthday. She was the second-to-last queen of Hawaii and fifty-five years old at the time. In her honor, the palace's cornerstone was laid with full Masonic rites. In older times, those rites would have involved a "foundation sacrifice," the act of burying a person alive inside that cornerstone so their spirit could forever guard the palace. While King Kalakaua was both a thirty-three-degree Mason and in charge of the construction, he preferred a more modern ceremony, choosing instead to insert a copper casket containing memorabilia of the day inside the cornerstone. Though that stone was lowered into place in full view of both the king and the assembled crowd, and the whole ceremony recorded in newspapers and in multiple Masonic accounts, a hundred years later, when restoration of the palace was undertaken, the cornerstone had vanished. "Architects poured over the blueprints, archeologists probed the foundations and the U.S. Army even assigned its metal detection squad to assist in the search—but the cornerstone has still not been located," wrote Rhoda Heckler in her guidebook *'Iolani Palace*. Whether or not this affair is an argument for human sacrifice in the name of good architecture remains something of an unanswered question, but it is worth pointing out that most of America's historic landmarks were built using similar, perhaps bloodthirsty, techniques.

The palace is a two-story rectangle parked in the middle of downtown Honolulu. The grounds are dominated by a pair of Indian banyan trees and a trim, square lawn. The building's style is American Florentine or Hawaiian Renaissance or something else that means big and fancy and imposing. Outside there are stone columns and rooftop towers. Inside are marble sinks and copper bathtubs. Originally gas chandeliers lit the rooms, but King Kalakaua was the first monarch to circumnavigate the globe and saw arc lighting demonstrated in Paris in 1881. Soon after, he had electricity installed in the palace, making it the first U.S. government building to venture into Edison's modern era. On the day I visited, one of the doyens explained this early technological adoption policy as "Um, Kalakáua was a bit of a geek."

The building itself was completed in 1882, but things didn't go so well from there. Eleven years after the palace became operational, in 1893, the Hawaiian monarchy was overthrown and a provisional government installed. In 1895, when dynamite was "found" buried in the royal garden, Queen Lili'uokalani was arrested for treason. She was imprisoned in her throne room, where she composed poems.

I live in sorrow.
Imprisoned.
You are my light.
Your glory my support.
Behold not with malevolence,
The sins of man.
But forgive.
And cleanse.

The queen was eventually released, but by 1989 the United States had annexed the whole Hawaiian archipelago and the glory days of the monarchy had gone the way of the dodo. About what happened to the sins of man, there is no record. I once asked Pake and Tom how they felt about the monarchy and the annexation and everything that happened afterward. After a little while Tom said, "It used to be a crime to cut down a coconut tree and not re-plant two seeds." He shook his head. "It's not a crime anymore." Pake composed a poem for the occasion.

> Donald Trump don't live here.
> Donald Trump don't want to live here.
> He's got to go thru us,
> If he wants to try.
> Oprah's buying up land
> Says she wants to give it to us.
> Go right ahead Oprah.
> We got plenty aloha for you.

I found the wind gourd on display in a small room in the palace basement. In less than ten minutes I had peppered three tour guides with several hundred questions. When they ran out of answers, I moved on to the guards. Since the wind gourd is both five hundred years old and made from koa, among the rarest and most expensive tropical hardwoods, perhaps it's understandable that the guards didn't much like answering the kinds of questions I was asking. In the end someone was sent to find the head curator. Not, as it turned out, because he had anything to tell me about the wind gourd, but because no one who worked there had ever seen anyone so excited about the wind gourd.

In its defense, at least by calabash standards, the wind gourd is immense: 34¾ inches high and 10 inches across. It was hand carved and later ornamented with two gold bands, one around its waist, the other around its neck. The bands were added in 1886 by an American cabinetmaker named William Miller and the newly jeweled jar presented to King Kalakaua on his fiftieth birthday, creating enough of a local sensation that the *Daily Bulletin* mentioned that "the jar is said to have been used centuries ago by chiefs, who, while fighting, spoke in it to the gods." Which strikes me as not the way the *New York Times* would have put it.

Miller also attached a gold plate to the gourd's lid, engraving it with a brief history: "The wind container of La'amaomao was in keeping of Hauna, personal attendant to Lonoikamakahiki I. It was passed on to Paka'a, a personal attendant of Kaewenuia'umi. It was placed in the royal burial cave of Hoaiki, on the sacred cliffs of Keoua, at Kawaawaloa, island of Hawaii, and received by King Kalakaua I on January 1, 1883, from Kaapana, caretaker of Hoaiku. The plaque on the wall beside the case read: Legend of the wind goddess La'amaomao tells of a container holding all the winds of the world. When its owner chanted the names of the winds, the calabash magically released them to fill the sails of voyaging canoes. Reading that, I felt about the same as I would have felt had I taken a tour of Monticello and come across the pen nibs Thomas Jefferson had used to authorize Lewis and Clark's expedition, and below them a small sign reading: These are the pen nibs of Thomas Jefferson. If you point them at true north and whisper *we the people* three times, you will never have to pay taxes again.

I stood beside that glass case for a very long time. The koa wood had been polished to a high sheen, the gold bands were luminous, the gourd itself long empty. I was told no one knows what happened to the bones of La'amaomao. I wondered about that. I wondered if somewhere out in the Pacific, sitting alone on a surfboard, was a man who called himself the Conductor and knew what happened to those bones. Maybe Tom Stone was right; maybe the tale I heard was the product of some surf-happy hippie too high to remember the right story, just high enough to remember the wrong one. Maybe remembering the wrong one was the point after all.

47

In the weeks since my arrival I had surfed with the crowds at Populars and the crowds at Canoes and the crowds at Queens and the crowds at Publics. I had ridden angry overhead slop at Diamond Head and regretted surfing leash-less at Rice Bowls. I had watched Tom Stone paddle his fourteen-foot hand-carved *olo* board out at Old Man's two days before watching him carry seventy-five pounds of that same board through a crowded mall and into Don Ho's restaurant because the valet had told him he wasn't allowed to park cars with surfboards on the roof. When Tom pointed out the board was really just a big plank of wood, the valet pointed out that it was a big plank of wood shaped like a surfboard. "It's also shaped like an enormous erect phallus," said Tom. "Can you park it with that on the roof?"

And then the surf went flat and stayed flat for three days, and then we started hearing rumors of waves heading for the other side of the island. There was talk this would be the North Shore's last big dance before shutting down for the season. There was talk it would be here tomorrow. How big? No one seemed to know. Pake thought maybe big. I had made a promise to Chris Marchetti at his funeral. There didn't seem to be any other options. In the morning, I was going surfing on the North Shore.

In Malaysia I learned that sleeping pills were among the most effective cures for a bad hangover and a hotel room positioned directly beside a gong-happy Buddhist temple. In Hawaii it took sleeping pills to fall asleep, but I was still up in those dread hours before dawn. The sheets seemed too hot, then too cold, the mattress too firm, then too soft. Neuroscientists link a racing mind to low levels of serotonin. Psychologists suggest the way to calm a racing mind is to imagine each thought as a leaf floating down a stream. Once I had defoliated much of Yellowstone National Park, I got out of bed and walked onto the hotel balcony.

My room was on the eleventh floor, so the view was all of Waikiki, spread out beneath a sky that was still mostly dark. In one direction was the night shadow of Diamond Head; in the other were the low lights of the high-rise hotels, the lights that crept out from behind closed curtains, the lights that meant that there were other people awake: the young lovers; the insomniacs; the sufferers of bad dreams; those who missed their children; those who missed much more; the businessmen checking in with far-off offices; the ones packing suitcases for the first flight out; the others unwilling to let yet another sunrise arrive unseen, whatever their reasons; the few, the far between. This is what passes for company in the dread hours when there is nothing to protect you from yourself.

In the pocket behind my driver's license was a folded-up piece of paper that contained one of the things I had learned watching *The West Wing*.

Voyager, in case it's ever encountered by extraterrestrials, is carrying photos of life on Earth, greetings in fifty-five languages, and a collection of music, from Gregorian chant to Chuck Berry, including "Dark Was the Night, Cold Was the Ground," by 1920s bluesman Blind Willie Johnson, whose stepmother blinded him at seven by throwing lye in his eyes after his father beat her for being with another man. He died penniless of pneumonia after sleeping bundled in wet newspapers in the ruins of his house that burned down, but his music just left the solar system.

I had placed it there years ago, when I was still sick enough to wonder if I would make it though to the other side. I have kept it there because I have learned that there is no other side. Illness brings along with it an unending consciousness of mortality, a permanent sense that the end game has already begun. More than a few researchers think that spiritual belief is nothing more than the brain's way of guarding against the idea of the inevitable.

Back when I was looking into the hows and whys of near-death experiences, the neuroscientist Michael Persinger told me that death was such an unfathomable idea that when most mammals are confronted with the possibility of their own mortality they freeze. Rats and cats and dogs and such, when given a severe electric shock for the first time, will become so afraid of the future that they can no longer move in the present. Since humankind has slightly more complex brains than these lower orders, we do not have to be shocked into understanding mortality; that shock is already with us. To get past that shock, our brains have devised exceptionally complicated strategies for survival: either the primarily Western notion of an afterlife or the primarily Eastern notion of reincarnation. In other words, belief is nothing more or less than a way to hope that someday our music will also leave the solar system.

I sat out on the balcony and reread that quote and thought it wasn't so much, what I wanted. I wanted today to be better than yesterday; I wanted tomorrow to be better than today. The words had become part of my strategy, perhaps not that different from my quest for the wind gourd, at least a way to grab my backpack and my surfboard and make it out of the hotel with the hope that tomorrow would be better than today.

Today we drove across the island and turned off Kamehameha Highway and into the gravel parking lot at Laniakea Beach Park. Less than three miles away was the town of Haleiwa. Less than four hundred yards offshore was one flank of a massive lava hammerhead. When northwest swells arrived at Laniakea, this hammerhead sectioned the wave into a series of skatepark ramps. When a rare north groundswell arrived, Laniakea produced a wave described by *Surfline* as "outrageously fast, with some super hollow sections. It requires a fine degree of judgment and a willingness to be picked off by wide swinging sets which are quite capable of returning the surfer to the original paddle out point." That paddle-out follows a channel that runs alongside the eastern edge of the point, before pouring over a shallower section of reef which usually gets crossed without incident. The kinds of incidents that happen at Laniakea have been known to leave scars.

That the waves didn't look much more than overhead and the swell more northwest than north did not change the fact that I stood on the beach and sensed a dire quiver. This was my limbic system teaming up with my fight-or-flight response to let me know that there have been times when I have done things like this before and they didn't work out so well. I had felt it on all those occasions when the past met the future in the now, and the only way to cope with the intersection was best expressed by the words *Bonzer Bonzai*.

So I did the only thing that made sense at the time: I asked La'amaomao for a little help and got in the damn water. The weeks of nonstop paddling had done me some good. I made time out to the lineup and took in the ochre mountains and the tall palms and then didn't give myself a chance to think things through any further. I caught my first wave on the North Shore about fifteen seconds after I reached the break. It wasn't much, head high, a bit faster than it looked from shore. I dropped down the face and felt the wave hit a shallower section and jacked an extra few feet at the last moment.

I made the drop and carried the speed through the bottom turn and rode that rise back into the sunlight as a gull flew overhead and the wave's next section opened its book of common prayer before me, and I knew that the thing that had scared me for almost half my life was suddenly behind me.

There were only a few guys out. We traded shorter lefts and longer rights for the better portion of an hour. I made sections and got rides and missed sections and got tumbled. It was maybe too good to last and didn't. By midmorning, the vibe wasn't quite as friendly as it had been for the first hour. Laniakea has a reputation as a town wave, meaning all the Honolulu locals with the kind of jobs that allow them to dash across the island at a moment's notice often dash here. These are folks who don't always like to share, and when they do decide to share, one of the better ways to not get another wave on the North Shore is to miss the one that's been given to you.

The wave that I was given was the set wave of the biggest set I had seen so far. The guy who gave it to me gave it to me because, paddle as he might, he couldn't seem to make it; so he swore once under his breath and pulled back and pointed at me. I remember thinking, If you don't make this wave there might not be another and if you do make this wave there might not be another. It was too big and I was too far inside, and the peak kept rising and I was spinning my board and popping to my feet. Then it was too late. There was no longer water beneath me. There was just empty space and the feeling of falling through empty space, and then it happened or didn't happen or whatever because the next thing I knew time had stopped.

It stopped just like it had stopped on that day in Santa Monica. The ocean froze, and the line of gauzy foam on the lip's edge turned crystalline, and a bubbling boil that meant shallow reef stilled and a gap where the water was silk smooth appeared. In that instant I felt that neurochemical rush that meant—*hey, buddy, pay attention, this is the stuff*—and then weighted the ball of my right foot and drove through that smooth section and onto the next and the next and on down the line. At the tail end of the ride, long after the speed of life had returned to normal, I realized that this had been my first wave on the North Shore. The other ones had been all warm-up and playacting, but this one had been the real deal. This one had some teeth.

I popped over the last section and dropped belly flat onto my board and found myself face-to-face with a sea turtle. He was big and green and maybe a foot away from me with his head peeking up through the surface of the water, eyes fixed on mine. He had a look like he'd been waiting all morning for me to show up and I was late and didn't I know that turtles keep a busy schedule. We sat and stared at each other for a long time before he turned and swam back beneath the waves. In the instant he disappeared, I heard Chris Marchetti's voice in my head. "Good job" was what he said. I might have imagined it. Good job was pretty high praise coming from Chris.

If you follow it backward, I had come to the North Shore and gone surfing and met a sea turtle because Chris Marchetti rode a peculiar five-fin thruster called a Bonzer. If you follow it forward, I got out of the water at Laniakea and went for breakfast at Café Haleiwa because James Fulbright had some friend-of-a-friend connection to the owner. The owner was a guy named Duncan Campbell. That was the extent of everything I knew about Duncan Campbell when we met. I didn't know that he had a brother named Malcolm or that in 1970, the two together shaped a radical three-finned, double-concave surfboard they described as "an entirely different reality in wave riding," and brought it to market adorned with slogans like "Always for Love, Never for Money." At the time they created it, a few prescient individuals urged the brothers to patent their idea and make a fortune, but true to their word they instead made their design specs public. Later, Duncan would say in

256

an interview: "We truly believe there is no original thought. All we claimed was that we were intuitive enough to combine existing ideas at a particular point in time to produce a superior surfboard design." Nor did I know that in 1982, Duncan and Malcolm modified their original design, adding two more fins, for a total of five. They gave the same name to both their three-fin and their five-fin boards. The name—Australian slang for "remarkable or wonderful"—was Bonzer.

I told Duncan and James about Chris and the Bonzer connection and my day at Laniakea. Duncan told me he taught a class on surfing and science and spirituality at a local community college. He had his own ideas about why time might freeze on a wave. "It's your brain's way of focusing," he said. "Of dropping you into the *now* by default. It doesn't really matter how you get there, but once you're there, well, there are certain fundamental properties inherent in the now. No time, no space. Just as rocks hold geological memory, waves hold oceanic memory. When surfing plunges you into the now, you have access to that information. It's like you're having a unique communication with the energy and information in a wave. Anyway, that's how we build our boards."

While much of the credit for the three-fin thruster went to an Australian named Simon Anderson, it has since been acknowledged that the triangulated system on the Campbell brothers' first Bonzer predates Anderson's contribution by a decade. The *Encyclopedia of Surfing* calls the three-fin design "the second most significant board design advance, following the shortboard revolution." It is worth pointing out that their five-fin thruster is starting to gather similar steam. It's also worth pointing out that Emily Dickinson once said, "If I feel physically that the top of my head were taken off, I know that is poetry."

When we drove away from Café Haleiwa, I watched the building until it vanished from my rearview mirror. That was the last I saw of the North Shore. Two days later I was on a plane back to California. Before I left, Joshua gave me a copy of Stuart Holmes Coleman's recent biography *Eddie Would Go: The Story of Eddie Aikau, Hawaiian Hero* to read on the flight home. It was a lovely gift, as there's none save Duke Kahanamoku so firmly connected to the spirit of wave riding as Eddie Aikau. It has been over a quarter century since his death, but the phrase EDDIE WOULD GO remains ubiquitous on bumper stickers and in conversations and island shorthand prayer for courage and grace and humility.

Born in Maui, Eddie moved to the island of Oahu in 1959. Of his debut at Waimea in 1966, *Surfer* magazine wrote, "He rode giant waves for over six hours without a break and when he finally left the water he was judged by most to have been one of the finest riders of the day." In 1967, after a string of deaths made it apparent that it was high time to station lifeguards on the North Shore, Eddie was one of the first hired. Because of his aversion to paperwork, no record remains of how many lives Eddie saved. Hundreds, perhaps thousands. It is known that no one ever died at Waimea on his watch.

On March 16, 1978, Eddie joined the crew of *Hokule'a* for its second voyage to Tahiti. The weather was not fine for sailing. The winds were gusting up to forty miles per hour, and there were ten-foot seas in the channels, but there was an enormous crowd and a considerable amount of media attention. Despite warnings from Eddie and several other crew members, the *Hokule'a* set out across the stormy Pacific. Five hours later, long after dark, the starboard hull sprung a leak and the ship capsized. Their emergency radio beacon was lost, their radio submerged. It was a rough night and a worse morning, and when there didn't seem any other options Eddie climbed atop the board he had brought along to surf in Tahiti and paddled for Lanai. The waves were enormous, the winds gale force, the island of Lanai some twenty miles away. Days later, a life vest was spotted by a rescue plane, but Eddie was never seen again.

At his funeral the Reverend Abraham Akaka said, "The open sea is to the Hawaiian people as the desert was to Moses and his people . . . a place to go and meet God."

In 1984, the first of what would soon become the Quicksilver in Memory of Eddie Aikau Big Wave Invitational was held at Sunset Beach. The contest has since been moved to Waimea, but the rules have not changed. Without twenty-foot surf, the competition cannot be held. That initial contest was won against long odds by Eddie's brother Clyde Aikau. Halfway across the ocean, I stumbled across the section in *Eddie Would Go* explaining Clyde's winning strategy. Joshua had circled it in pen so I was sure to notice.

> During the finals of the Quicksilver Contest, Clyde saw two turtles swimming out beyond the lineup. In the face of such huge waves, they seemed calm and playful like Eddie . . . used to be. Staring at the graceful creatures, a voice inside him said, "Follow the turtles." As a native Hawaiian steeped in mana, Clive believed that animals could take the form of *'aumakua*, or spiritual guardians, so he listened to his instincts and followed them. Knowing that positioning was critical in big surf, he paddled toward the turtles way past the lineup. When he was far beyond the other competitors, Clyde suddenly saw the biggest wave of the day rise up on the horizon and swallow the sky. He turned his board around, started stroking for the beast and then dropped more than forty feet down its rushing face. Crouched just ahead of its rushing maw, Clyde rode the wave across the Bay to the inside section until it died out. The crowds on the beach and the overlooking cliff shouted with excitement. When he finally made it back out, Clyde followed the turtles once again. Another set came rolling in, and he rode the mammoth wave all the way in to the shore.

I don't know what to believe about the turtle I met at Lani-akea, but I have come to feel my promise to Chris has been ful-filled. In *The White Album,* Joan Didion wrote "We tell ourselves stories in order to live" and then proceeded to tell a story about a time in her life when the stories she told herself began to fail. Maybe that's how it is for all of us. Maybe that's how things go. Maybe we tell ourselves such stories right up until the moment we can no longer tell ourselves such stories. We believe the earth is flat until we believe it is round. We believe in a geocentric universe until we believe in a heliocentric universe. We believe that heliocentric uni-verse governed by a fixed logic until we believe that heliocentric universe all relative. We believe the speed of light is inviolate, until we find out that entangled particles could outpace the speed of light. Scientists now believe that the quantum world is a world of possibility. They believe that our most fundamental level of reality is not any one firm reality, rather the possibility of an infinite num-ber of possibilities. We cannot find the cornerstone of our founda-tion because everything and nothing are the cornerstones of our foundation. We live in a world of magnificent maybe. And every now and again someone rattles the bones of the past in the direc-tion of the future in the hopes that a wave will rise.

Acknowledgments

This one was definitely a team effort. *Discover, GQ, Men's Journal, Blue, Bikini, LA Weekly* and *Wired* all published sections of this book in other forms. I'm grateful to my editors—Sarah Richardson, Jim Nelson, Peter Frank, Amy Schrier, Rob Hill, Joe Donnelly and Mark Robinson—for their wisdom and expertise. An immeasurable thanks to my agent Paul Bresnick, my editor Kathy Belden and everyone at Bloomsbury. A lot of wonderful people showed tremendous patience and offered great advice along the way: Joshua Lauber, Michael Wharton, Tom Foster, Jori Finkel, Sheerly Avni, Adam Aaronson, Micah Abrams, Burk Sharpless, Dawn Miller, Kaja Perina, Matt Lian, Kevin Daniels, Liz Arnold, Michael Reardon, Tom Tapp, Shannon Weber, Matt and Julie Kotler, Brad and Jenny Kotler. Howard Shack and Chris Marchetti taught me to surf, and Andrea Pesce got me back in the water. Melvin Morse, Willoughby Britton, Robert White and Andrew Newberg helped make sense of some pretty mystifying neuroscience. The New Zealand tourism board redefined hospitality. Tom Stone and Pake Aw Mow opened their lives to me. And finally, to my mom and dad for never wavering. Thank you all.